AMERICA'S
QUILTS AND COVERLETS

AMERICA'S QUILTS AND COVERLETS

by

Carleton L. Safford and Robert Bishop

WEATHERVANE BOOKS

NEW YORK

Color plate, page 1: Appliqué quilt, c. 1860, Pennsylvania. 94¼″ × 79½″. (Mr. and Mrs. John Gordon)

Color plate, page 2 and *color plate, above:* Enlarged details from Baltimore Album quilt illustrated on pages 148–149. (Privately owned)

Color plate, page 5: Enlarged detail from appliqué and patchwork quilt illustrated on pages 168–169. (Privately owned)

Color plate, page 7: Enlarged detail from appliqué quilt illustrated on page 1.

Library of Congress Catalog Card Number: 72-82707
All rights reserved under International and Pan-American Copyright Conventions.
This edition published by Weathervane Books
a division of Barre Publishing Company, Inc.
by arrangement with E. P. Dutton & Co., Inc.

a   b   c   d   e   f   g   h

Printed and bound in Spain by
Novograph S. A. and Roner S. A., Madrid.
D. L.: M. 27.173 - 1974

CONTENTS

ACKNOWLEDGMENTS

The authors wish to express their gratitude to the many persons involved in the production of this book. More than three hundred institutions, historical societies, and museums of decorative arts were contacted and requested to inform us of pertinent material in their collections. They were most generous in their response. Private collectors and dealers were equally generous in permitting us to photograph and illustrate unpublished pieces. Grateful acknowledgment is hereby made to all for their invaluable help.

Collectors and Dealers: Mr. and Mrs. Leonard Balish, Englewood, New Jersey; Mr. and Mrs. Whitney Balliett; Mr. and Mrs. James B. Boone, Jr.; Gary C. Cole, New York; Allan L. Daniel, New York; Gary R. Davenport; Mr. and Mrs. Edward S. George; Cora Ginsburg; Lewis B. Rockwell, Ginsburg & Levy, Inc., New York; Rhea Goodman: Quilt Gallery, Inc., New York; Mr. and Mrs. John Gordon, New York; Mr. and Mrs. Michael D. Hall; Mrs. Barbara Johnson; Mrs. Jacob M. Kaplan; Mr. and Mrs. Foster McCarl, Jr.; Sarah Melvin; Mr. and Mrs. Durand R. Miller; Mr. and Mrs. Donald Morris; Mr. and Mrs. Peter P. Nitze; Julia Boyer Reinstein; Marguerite Riordan, Stonington, Connecticut; Ryther House Gallery, Bernardston, Massachusetts; George Schoellkopf: The Peaceable Kingdom, Ltd., New York; Mr. and Mrs. Walter E. Simmons; Mr. and Mrs. Walter E. Simmons, II; Betty Sterling: Brainstorm Farm, Randolph, Vermont; Mr. and Mrs. Don Walters; Alan J. Zuch: The Williamsville Inn, West Stockbridge, Massachusetts; Several Anonymous Private Collectors.

Institutions: Abby Aldrich Rockefeller Folk Art Collection, Williamsburg, Virginia; Arthur W. Leibundguth, Director, Antiquarian and Landmarks Society, Inc., of Connecticut, Hartford, Connecticut; Elizabeth Ann Coleman, Department of Decorative Arts, The Brooklyn Museum, Brooklyn, New York; Mrs. Boudinot S. Davis, Curator, Baltimore County Historical Society, Inc., Cockeysville, Maryland; Mrs. John P. Renick, Curator, Bedford Historical Society, Bedford, New York; Harriet Ropes Cabot, Curator, The Bostonian Society, Boston, Massachusetts; Elizabeth H. Sias, Curator, Bucks County Historical Society, Doylestown, Pennsylvania; Dr. Carol Macht, Curator, and Mary L. Meyer, Cincinnati Art Museum, Cincinnati, Ohio; Martha G. Thomas, Department of Textiles, The Cleveland Museum of Art, Cleveland, Ohio; The Colonial Williamsburg Foundation, Williamsburg, Virginia; The Connecticut Historical Society, Hartford, Connecticut; Mrs. David Siedenburg, Cortland County Historical Society, Inc., Cortland, New York; Julia Boyer Reinstein, Erie County Historical Federation, Cheektowaga, New York; Elisabeth S. Donaghy, Director-Curator, Daughters of the American Revolution Museum, Washington, D.C.; Huldah M. Payson, Curator, Essex Institute, Salem, Massachusetts; Genesee Country Museum, Mumford, New York; Greenfield Village and Henry Ford Museum, Dearborn, Michigan; Mary Claire Peden, Manager-Curator, Gunston Hall, Lorton, Virginia; Ruth Zalusky Thorstenson, Curator, Hennepin County Historical Society, Minneapolis, Minnesota; Charles F. Hummel, Curator, and Karol A. Schmiegel, Assistant Registrar, The Henry Francis du Pont Winterthur Museum, Winterthur, Delaware; Margery Howe, Historic Deerfield, Inc., Deerfield, Massachusetts; Eliza W. McCready, Museum Curator, Historical Society of Delaware, Wilmington, Delaware; Marvell A. Hart, Keeper of Collections, Honolulu Academy of Arts, Honolulu, Hawaii; Hudson River Museum, Yonkers, New York; Kentucky Historical Society, Frankfort, Kentucky; Ladies' Hermitage Association, Hermitage, Tennessee; William L. Warren, Director, The Litchfield Historical Society, Litchfield, Connecticut; Edgar de N. Mayhew, Director, Lyman Allyn Museum, New London, Connecticut; Mary Merwin, The Massillon Museum, Massillon, Ohio; Frances Gruber, Assistant Curator, The American Wing, The Metropolitan Museum of Art, New York; Christine Meadows, Curator, The Mount Vernon Ladies' Association of the Union, Mount Vernon, Virginia; Larry Salmon, Curator of Textiles, Museum of Fine Arts, Boston, Massachusetts; Jack T. Ericson, Curator of Decorative Arts, The Newark Museum, Newark, New Jersey; Doris P. Purvis, Assistant Curator, New Hampshire Historical Society, Concord, New Hampshire; James J. Heslin, Director, The New-York Historical Society, New York; Evelyn F. Anderson, Oaklands Association, Inc., Murfreesboro, Tennessee; Daniel B. Reibel, Curator, Old Economy Village, Ambridge, Pennsylvania; Elizabeth S. Winton, Executive Secretary, Old Gaol Museum, York, Maine; Judith Wragg Chase, Curator, The Old Slave Mart Museum, Charleston, South Carolina; Thomas S. Eader, The Peale Museum, Baltimore, Maryland; Elise McGarvey, Curator of Costumes and Textiles, Philadelphia Museum of Art, Philadelphia, Pennsylvania; Blanche K. Reigle, Director, Pennsylvania Farm Museum of Landis Valley, Lancaster, Pennsylvania; Lynn Springer, St. Louis Art Museum, St. Louis, Missouri; Sterling D. Emerson, Director, Shelburne Museum, Inc., Shelburne, Vermont; Lois R. Dater, Curator, The Stamford Historical Society, Inc., Stamford, Connecticut; Mildred J. Davis, Consulting Curator, Valentine Museum, Richmond, Virginia; J. Herbert Callister, Curator of Textiles and Costumes, Wadsworth Atheneum, Hartford, Connecticut; Cecilia Steinfeldt, Curator of History, Witte Memorial Museum, San Antonio, Texas.

Other Individuals: Charles R. Counts, artist, Rising Fawn, Georgia; Jean Ray Laury, author of *Quilts and Coverlets,* Clovis, California; Irene Preston Miller, Croton-on-Hudson, New York; Florence Pettit, author of *America's Printed and Painted Fabrics,* Glenbrook, Connecticut; Ruth E. Wollet, President, Colonial Coverlet Guild of America

Photographs not furnished by participating museums have been made by Charles T. Miller, Carl Molotka, and Rudolph Rusicska, all of the Henry Ford Museum; by Douglas Armsden of Kittery Point, Maine; and by Arthur Vitols of Helga Photo Studio in New York City. Their fine work and infinite patience is deeply appreciated. Clyde W. Poland of Ann Arbor, Michigan, acted as researcher and correspondent in identifying material furnished by public and private sources. He was also an invaluable assistant in proofreading sessions. Patricia Coblentz was a most able Editorial Assistant. We are grateful to them all.

CARLETON L. SAFFORD
ROBERT BISHOP

8

INTRODUCTION

The purpose of this book is to illustrate and discuss the great variety and beautiful design of the bedcoverings created by past generations of American women. To this end we have assembled here photographs of the many types of quilts and coverlets made since homes were first established in America in the seventeenth century. These illustrations include outstanding examples of design and workmanship from both public and private collections, many of which are published in this volume for the first time. Accompanying these is a layman's nontechnical account of the development of styles, materials, and needlework.

As a nation we have been slow to recognize and appreciate our ancestors' great accomplishments in the decorative arts. It is an extraordinary fact that not until 1924, with the opening of The American Wing at The Metropolitan Museum of Art in New York, the most important museum in America, were the American decorative arts given major display space in a museum. Also, the first books on antiques written in the 1920's were mostly reminiscent and romantic, as well as being poorly authenticated and poorly illustrated. In recent years, however, the enthusiastic appreciation of our rich heritage of design and craftsmanship has found expression in many handsome books in the fields of American architecture, furniture, painting, silver, glass, pottery, etc. To this growing library we now add *America's Quilts and Coverlets,* hoping thus to show the wealth of beauty one can discover in America's textiles.

The source material available for the study of textiles and their uses is small. Inventories and diaries mention various types of cloth by name, but include few descriptions, and since textiles quickly became worn, they were usually destroyed rather than being stored in an attic. Most that has been written on the subject has been repetitive and based on supposition or unrelated facts. With the exception of the samplers made by young girls, which were generally dated and inscribed with the maker's name, few examples of early needlework incorporate specific information for classifying it until after the middle of the nineteenth century. However, the data for examples of textiles included in museum collections is relatively trustworthy, since some of these have found their way into

1 (opposite page), 1a (right), 1b (overleaf). Appliqué bedcover, c. 1800, made by Sarah Furman Warner of Greenfield Hill, Connecticut. 105″ × 84″. Accented with embroidery, this folk-art masterpiece in the appliqué style is wonderfully pictorial. It undoubtedly represents the buildings and the citizens of the small New England village in which it was created. The wide border composed of vines and birds and urns filled with flowers has been executed with unusual skill. (Henry Ford Museum)

2 (above), 2a, 2b, and 2c (overleaf). Appliqué coverlet on linen, c. 1800, New York, made by Ann Walgrave Warner for Phebe Warner. 104″ × 90″. The materials used for appliqué are block-printed cottons, calicoes, and India chintzes. Embroidery outlines the patches, using chain, stem, and buttonhole stitches. The hair of the figures is worked in French knots of colored silks. (The Metropolitan Museum of Art, Gift of Catherine E. Cotheal, 1938)

collections because of their association with important families, and because curators have increasingly come to recognize the importance of preserving, studying, and documenting American textiles as fully as possible.

With English examples as a guide, it is possible to reconstruct the history of American bedcoverings because of the similarities in style. Styles in America lagged several decades behind those of England and Europe because the earliest English settlers and the emigrants from other regions of Europe were too busy gaining a foothold in the New World to worry about the latest fashions. Strength and warmth were of chief importance. But when the time finally arrived for a "dressing up," the housewife remembered what she had seen at home, and recreated it in America. Thus our early eighteenth-century style was apt to be late seventeenth century in inspiration. This time lag lasted into the nineteenth century, when more rapid interchange through printed patterns and style sheets brought us up to date with contemporary European styles.

The differences between the design of household articles in America and abroad was generally due to a lack of skill in design and great limitations of materials. Whatever might be lacking in fineness of detail was made up for in a sense of simplified line and form, and there has always been this feeling for simplicity in American decorative styles. This was not as true in the cities where fashions were first received from abroad and fine materials were available, but it was very apparent in the small towns and villages where rural Americanism asserted itself early. This self-taught, experimental, folk-art quality in American decorative arts is both highly prized and studied today.

Elizabethan design was a strong influence on our early needlework: scrolls, scallopings, bold plant forms, and whole areas being filled with embroidery, as can be found in early tapestries. The East India Company and its goods added the Oriental look: the "Tree of Life," tropical trees and flowers, exotic birds. Peonies, chrysanthemums, and carnations were added from Persia. The artichoke (coming perhaps from Italy) became an especially popular motif in weaving because of its symmetry. The needlewoman cared not that she mixed palms and oaks, or that she had pomegranates and pineapples growing from the same tree as apples and cherries. Pattern books containing all these, and many more elements, were popular all over Europe, to be worked in crewel, cross-stitch, petit-point, lace, furniture inlay, and even architecture. While some of these design books inevitably found their way to America, very few would have been available in our rural areas; thus the country needlewoman depended largely on her imagination for her masterful designs. America reached its height in design and native craftsmanship, as we shall see in the succeeding chapters, from about 1725 to 1900.

The foregoing discussion has been involved with "design" as a term, but with no special understanding of design as such. We have named some of the motifs which can make up a design. A design can be good; it can also be poor. By learning what it is, we can distinguish between good and bad design. The *American Heritage Dictionary of the English Language* calls it "invention and disposition of the forms, parts, or details of something according to a plan." More clearly stated for our purposes, it comprises "pleasing" combinations of lines, masses, and colors. Plan is "harmony." We put design to work as we learn to recognize the reaction of one element against another to enhance the whole, to make it individual, and finally to make it part of a composition. A ballet, a piece of jewelry, a painting, and an opera can all be examples of harmonious composition. Today's non-art is the exception; it is also the opposite of design. To be a master designer we must put these principles of design successfully to work, in order to make the layman aware of it and to excite his appreciation. We should not design just for our own satisfaction!

Applied to the field of antiques, design becomes good or bad according to personal taste and according to the period of its creation. There is a general feeling among antiques collectors that the eighteenth century represents the best of native American design, with the nineteenth century running a close second.

Of course, age alone is not necessarily a built-in guarantee of good design, but the eighteenth century produced relatively few mistakes. Of the hundreds of early houses that remain along the eastern seaboard, few can be adversely criticized. Roof lines, chimneys, placement of windows and doors, ells, and lean-tos—all seem to be the perfect statement of an artist, yet few of the early builders were trained architects, few had even seen any printed material on construction and detailing, except as it was brought from Europe; and our early architecture did not take its inspiration from European examples. It used only the details that were suited to a new country and a new way of life. Cabinetmakers also adapted imported ideas, but made few mistakes in their adaptations. And in textiles, embroidery, and weaving, the early American housewife exhibited the same innate sense of good taste in her decorations for the home, the beauty and charm of which still captivate us today.

One of the most fascinating subjects for study in our early textiles are the dyes used to color them. The Old Slater Mill in Pawtucket, Rhode Island, which began spinning cotton in 1793, is now a museum where forty species of dye plants are grown together with as many as eight plants of fibrous textures for weaving. Another exhibit of early sources for natural dyes is the garden at the Harlow Old Fort House in Plymouth, Massachusetts. The use of early mordants, the results of natural experiments with iron and salt, is also illustrated

here. The American housewife of the earliest period discovered she could not remove rust spots from her linens, and about the same time she was constantly dyeing wool indigo blue for clothing. She found that her color became darker and clearer in an iron kettle than when she used any other type of dye-pot. To prove this she added nails and filings from the blacksmith's shop to her kettle. Other mordants were soon discovered. Colors produced at home were not bright. The natural vegetable dyes produced all that seemed needed. These colors are often listed: olive, snuff, bat-wing, drab, liver, sad-color, dove, lead, slate, cinnamon, copper. Salts, alum, and copperas became common agents to set the color. Indigo remained the commonest color for a hundred years, however, because it was permanent, and was available at small cost from a country store. The story of the indigo dye-pot on the kitchen hearth in every household on the Atlantic coast is often repeated. It needed to be kept warm to ferment and keep its "strength."

Bright-colored fabrics were imported, for the dyes did not become available until later. Venetian red was a well-guarded secret. Black from European sources was the best, and a purple remained unequaled until our own invention of aniline. Yellows were abundant from several sources, together with mordants to deepen or redden them. In 1856 mauve, the first coal-tar color, was discovered, and from this discovery came our synthetic colors of today.

The gradual development of successful textile factories in America in the late eighteenth and early nineteenth centuries caused an inevitable decline in the amount of home-fashioned textiles; yet they continued to survive in the country districts, particularly in Kentucky and Tennessee. Let us by no means forget "Weaver Rose," a barefoot character living in Kingston, Rhode Island, who became something of a tradition in New England in the later nineteenth century. He was sought after for his Overshot coverlets, with more orders than he could fill. He also became a famous maker of coverlet designs that were written on brown wrapping paper, and in 1912 he formed an organization that became The Colonial Weaver's Association.

Weaver Rose's spirit—indeed, the whole strong tradition of needlework and weaving produced in the home—is now enjoying a great resurgence of interest in modern America. It is a happy note with which to close these introductory words.

3, 3a (above), 3b (opposite). Bed rug, signed and dated "M 1722 A." The initials
are those of Mary Avery of North Andover, Massachusetts. 98″ × 88″. The
chevron or flamestitch design of the "drops" probably indicates a European model.
(Essex Institute)

THE BED RUG

The origin of the bed rug as a bedcover in America has yet to be fully explained. Antiquarians have expressed various opinions, but no one theory has been sustained. When The Magazine *Antiques* printed, in November 1927, a first, very brief article by its then famous editor, Homer Eaton Keyes, the "bed rugg" was a one-of-a-kind discovery. Subsequent authors of books on textiles in the 1930's were either afraid to mention bed rugs at all or referred to them in such vague terms as "wool-on-wool embroideries," "hooked rugs," etc. And all believed that bed rugs were to be found only in the general area of the Connecticut River Valley. Since quite a few bed rugs have now been discovered, it is possible for us to establish a few generalities about them.

The word "rugg" is probably directly descended from the Swedish "rugge," meaning "coarse" or "rough." In English, a "rug" was a thick cloak. In Finnish, a word in very early use was *ryijy,* meaning rug, and in Finland rugs were used as bedcovers. It is interesting to learn that there are some ancient bedcovers on exhibit in the Norsk Folk Museum near Oslo and in the Hanseatiske Museum in Bergen. These examples are very similar to the bed rugs we know are American. The Norwegian rugs have a more "felted" or matted quality than American ones, however, probably due to their age and the type of wool used in them. According to the Oxford English Dictionary, "Rugge" means a coarse coverlet in Norwegian. Also, in English journals, diaries, and inventories, the word "rugg" meant a coarse woolen material for clothing or a "thick woolen stuff" used as a coverlet. A dictionary often found in homes of the well-to-do in the eighteenth century is Nathaniel Bailey's *Dictionarium Brittanicum: Complete Universal Etymological English Dictionary,* London, 1730. In this "rugg" is defined as a shaggy coverlet for a bed.

The following are interesting early references to bed rugs.

In 1630 Governor John Winthrop wrote from Massachusetts to his son in England "to bring a store of Coarse Rugges, bothe to use and to sell."

About the same time in the cold New World, Lord Baltimore warned those coming to these shores to "take one rugg for a bed" and a "course Rugg to use at sea."

In 1636 the ship "William and John" came to Massachusetts from England with 240 yards of rugs for beds.

Thus it appears that each migration from Europe came bundled in bed rugs, especially those coming from cold countries. Bed rugs were often called "Biscay" rugs when loaded onto ships in Poland, France, Ireland, or England. If coming from Spain, they were termed "Bilbao." One hundred years later (c. 1740) they were still advertised as a guard against the cold in the Colonies. "Bristol" rugs and "Torrington" rugs from England were advertised in Williamsburg, Virginia. Few, if any, of these imported rugs have survived the centuries. One was discovered under a carpet, still guarding against cold drafts in an old house in Vermont!

There are a number of interesting references in old inventories to New England bed rugs, and we are illustrating some five examples here. All are similar in one respect: the whole spread is covered with design, and most are "worked" on a coarse woolen homespun, often called "say" in the eighteenth century. This background is usually a butternut-dyed, heavy, plain woolen. The colors in the large, flamboyant designs are usually brilliant even today, for the dyes were well set. Whereas indigo predominated in plain fabric covers, there is a tendency for bed rugs to be made in warm colors, possibly because such colors made one *feel* warmer!

Our American bed rugs are usually initialed and dated by their makers. One of the earliest known examples is owned by the Essex Institute in Salem, Massachusetts, and is inscribed "M 1722 A" (figures 3, 3a). It was made by a Mary Avery of North Andover, Massachusetts. It is worked in wool on a homespun linen in a bold, unschooled, original design. Very few have been found worked on linen, fewer still on silk; whatever materials were on hand was probably the prime consideration. Some of these rugs are "knotted" as were the so-called rag floor rugs of the late nineteenth century, where rags were tied through the weave of the background material to form a design. Most are done with a hand-spun wool, coarse and nubby, somewhat like the hooked rug that

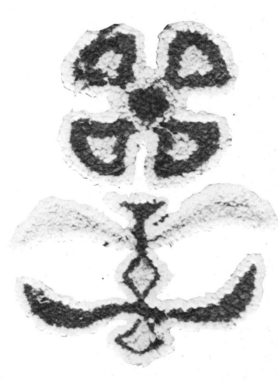

4 (above). Bed rug, dated 1809 and initialed "MB."
100½" × 100½". A well-developed design of carnations.
(The Metropolitan Museum of Art, Rogers Fund, 1913)

5 (above). Bed rug, signed "Sara Denny," but undated.
97" × 87". Evidently an original design. It is loosely constructed in warm beiges, yellows, and light reds. (Shelburne
Museum, Inc.)

was to follow more than a hundred years later, when it also became fashionable to cover floors.

In a study of 109 rural inventories for the years 1675 to 1775 for Suffolk County near Boston, Abbott Lowell Cummings cites 65 references to bed rugs. He also gives 62 references to "coverlets" and 6 to "counterpains." That these various forms of bedcoverings coexisted is a known fact, but we cannot be as certain of the exact years when each type was popular.

Here are typical extracts from these early inventories.

Dorchester, May 1675
in the parlor one feather bed and two bolsters 1 pare of shee 2 blankets one old green Rugg Curtaines valens and bedstead.

Roxbury, November 1675
in the lower rooms one old rugg one cradle rugg cradle pillows and foure cushins.

Roxbury, 1676
in the little room one standing bedsteed with a ffeatherbed boulsters, pillow, blankets, coverlit and curtanes.
in the chamber two bedsteeds and two beds, the one a ffeatherbed, the other fflocks and ffeathers together with 5 blankets and a Rugge.

Dedham, 1677
in the chambr, one bedsteed the bed cord one feather bed one bolster one blanket one Rug and a coverlit. Several goud green woosted Ruggs one red rug. [It must be noted that "ruggs" are always seemingly of one color, and with no pattern. This is probably due, however, to the carelessness of the officer making the accounting, and the haste in finishing the long lists of properties.]

Dedham, 1691
In ye bed rhome a bed bolster and pillows a darnick worked coverlid another coverlid gray streaked curtains vallians canope bedsteed and straw bed one blanket. [The "darnick" worked coverlid is probably a crewel-type cover where some of the background was left showing.]

It is interesting to find in the following inventories that bed rugs are becoming intermixed with what are obviously other types of bedcovers.

Dorchester, 1732
in Stoughton's chamber 1 Bedstead and curtains 1 old quilt 3 blankets. [When rugs and quilts are listed in the inventory for one room, one was intended for winter, one for summer. Gradually, the quilt supplanted the rug.]

Dorchester, 1763

In the Blue Chamber 1 Callico quilt [also] in the kitchen Chamber 2 Rugs and 1 blanket.

Milton, 1770

In the Back Chamber 2 Beds and bolsters 1 Rug Quilt Blankets 1 course Lid 1 Silk Quilt 1 pair Blankets 1 chair Bed and pillow Coverlid Blankets.

Roxbury, 1770

House furniture in the Garret five beds Underbeds Bedsteds and Cords five Ruggs seven Blanketts.

Finally, in a Roxbury inventory of 1774: "in the third room, a carpet on the floor." This is the first reference to any type of floor covering. As late as 1792 George Washington ordered a bed rug for the new executive mansion in Philadelphia. Perhaps he had become accustomed to using such a coverlet because of the one willed to his mother in 1721.

A particularly interesting bed rug (figure 15) of later date (1773) is the property of the Museum of the Daughters of the American Revolution in Washington. It was made by Polly (usually known as "Molly") Stark, the wife of General John Stark, for his niece Polly at the time of the latter's marriage to James Lathrop. This bed rug is seven feet square, made of coarse homespun wool raised, cleaned, and dyed on the outskirts of Derryfield, New Hampshire (now Manchester). It is woven in two lengths and seamed through the center. Mrs. Stark probably created her own pattern, a bold design of acanthus scrolls and carnation-like flowers and buds. She seems to have taken several strands of wool and pushed them together through the interstices of the coarse blanketing, almost as in hooking. The stitches are even and the result is a soft, deep pile. A great-granddaughter of Polly Lathrop presented it to the Society for safekeeping. The colors have softened with time, and range from a tan through browns to a tawny red.

A still later bed rug that we illustrate belongs to Cora Ginsburg and represents a development in style (figure 13). The coverlet is dated 1802 and was made by Philena McCall. The carnations in this design have become thistle-like, perhaps denoting a Scotch background. The McCall rug is stronger in conception and the colors are more contrasting than in the Stark example.

The bed rug owned by the Wadsworth Atheneum in Hartford (figures 14, 14a) shows quite a different approach in its design and technique. Here wool yarn is worked in a series of chain-stitch lines that circle about the main motifs of the design until the entire ground is filled. It has been worked in three shades of blue on a creamy white background and signed "Hannah Pearl." Unlike the other examples cited here, this bed rug bears no date.

6 (above). Bed rug, dated 1819 and initialed "N C." 97″ × 93″. A conventional but well-planned pattern in blues and browns on a beige ground. (The Henry Francis du Pont Winterthur Museum)

7 (above). Bed rug, dated 1807 and initialed "E L." 100″ × 95″. A design with flowers arranged in orderly fashion, a repetition of the carnation form, which is common to bed rugs. (Shelburne Museum, Inc.)

8, 8a (above). Bed rug, dated 1783 and initialed "W R B." 90″ × 87″. Worked on a heavy wool in yarns of blues, white, and dark brown. Rows of lunettes and the double-cusped border on three sides is unusual. (Winterthur Museum)

9 (right), 9a (opposite). Bed rug, dated 1790 and initialed "R G" for the Greer family of Norwich, Connecticut. 88″ × 85″. The design closely resembles that of figure 8, and the method of "sewing" the wool yarn in place is also similar. (The Brooklyn Museum)

10, 10a (above). Bed rug, signed "Mary Foot" and dated 1778, Connecticut. 83½″ × 77½″. Worked on a linen homespun in yarns using an all-over running stitch. The background is beige with the design in blues. (Winterthur Museum)

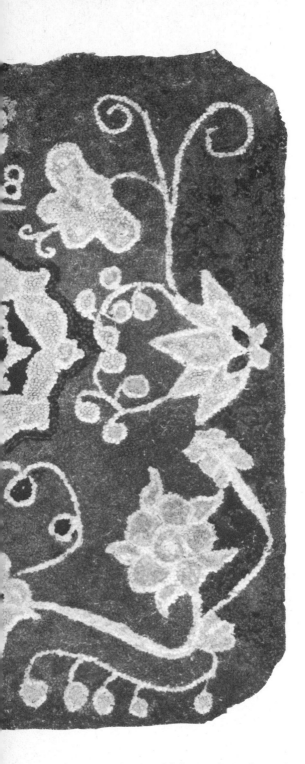

12 (below). Bed rug, dated and initialed "E H 1779," possibly for Elihu Hyde of Chelsea, Vermont. 95″ × 89″. This is one of the earliest "discoveries" to be termed a "bed rug." Wool yarn is "sewn" through wool blanketing, and the loops are sheared, except for the initials and date. The design is in faded blues and green against tan. (The New-York Historical Society)

11 (center). Bed rug, dated 1748 and initialed "F B."
88″ × 83″. Worked on a coarse linen with compact loops of thick woolen yarn "sewn" in a coarse, primitive floral pattern. The design is beige and white on a medium blue ground. (Winterthur Museum)

13 (left). Bed rug, dated 1802 and signed "Philena McCall." 100″ × 92″. Brilliant in its design and its use of color, this is one of the finest examples of the "hooked" type of bed rug. (Cora Ginsburg)

14 (right). Bed rug, signed "Hannah Pearl." It was probably made in the eighteenth century in central Connecticut. 90″ × 81″. The rug is worked on a wool ground in a single width. It is solidly covered with stem stitching of six-ply yarns in blues against cream. Remnants remain of the maker's name, but the area has been "unpicked" with only traces remaining. (Wadsworth Atheneum)

15 (left). Bed rug, made c. 1773 by "Molly" Stark, wife of General John Stark, of Derryfield (now Manchester), New Hampshire. 84″ × 84″. The colors are somewhat faded, but this rug is still a beautiful concert of earth colors. (Museum of the Society of the Daughters of the American Revolution)

16 (right). Bed rug, dated and initialed "R P 1805" for Rachel Packard, of Jericho, Vermont. 93½″ × 90″. Worked on wool homespun, the background is made of finely spun yarn, while the bright yarns making the design are somewhat coarser in texture. The loops of the "hooked" designs are short. (Henry Ford Museum)

17 (above). Bed rug, undated and unsigned. 85″ × 74″. Little
is known about the origin of this example, but the well-planned
design indicates it was created by an experienced craftsman.
(Old Gaol Museum)

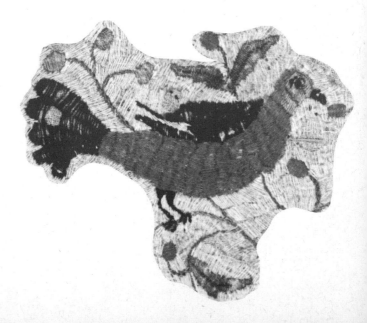

18 (below), 18a (opposite, below). Bed rug, dated 1779 and signed "Amy Williams" of Connecticut. 92¼″ × 81½″. The ground of this coverlet is coarse wool homespun, and the entire surface is covered in satin stitch in multicolored wools. (The Cleveland Museum of Art, Gift of Gardner Abbott, Jr., Luther Abbott, Willard Abbott, and Julian Abbott)

LINSEY-WOOLSEY

Forty years of public interest in restoration and decoration of eighteenth-century American homes has made the term "linsey-woolsey" quite well known. In the 1930's I visited an antique shop in the Cherry Valley area of New York State and found there a neatly folded watermelon-pink linsey-woolsey spread. I asked the dealer what it was and the price, and learned I could buy the piece for $10.00! It had been discovered in a local attic carefully wrapped in mothproof paper, and labeled: "Preserved by —— who came to —— from Vermont in 1835." The dealer did not know what to call the coverlet because it was made of quilted wool, and she was familiar only with nineteenth-century forms of quilting.

Linsey-woolsey has two important characteristics in a study of bed coverings. First, it is a quilted spread, probably the earliest type of quilting in the Colonies; and second, it is made of wool and is nearly always found in the country, especially in cold regions.

In the *American Heritage Dictionary of the English Language* the term linsey-woolsey is defined as being "a coarse fabric of cotton or linen woven with wool." It is not necessarily, therefore, always a combination of linen and wool, as the name would imply. There has been a tendency, in fact, to discount as variants from the norm the spreads that are made of cotton and wool. The name linsey-woolsey is derived from Middle English "lynsy wolsye," and "lynsy" comes from Lindsay, a village in Suffolk, England, where the fabric originated. The term does not show up in many inventories, and when it does, it usually connotes a fabric used in heavy clothing and quilted petticoats. Our use of the term "linsey-woolsey" today, however, refers to a heavy, warm, quilted bedcover usually made to hang to the floor, with the corners cut out at the foot so as to fit the tall four-posted beds of the eighteenth century. Beds of this period were both short and wide: short, because people slept with many bolsters; wide, because a bed rarely "slept" fewer than three people (and in some cases four or five). The coverlets made for these beds are consequently very large.

Quilting came to Europe from the Orient when the Crusaders discovered how comfortable the Turks were with two or three thicknesses of fabric "quilted" together under their armor. In northern Europe they soon took advantage of the additional warmth afforded by two pieces of fabric with a thin layer of wool between, "joined with stitching" to hold all in place. Quilted linsey-woolsey petticoats came to America with the first settlers, but the spreads did not. We have no recorded dates for linsey-woolsey coverlets since they were rarely initialed or dated. I have known of only one such example, and it was dated much later than one would expect.

Linsey-woolsey came naturally to be the chief product of northern homes. The coarse linen that became its warp was made from flax grown in the Colonies. This same "tow" or homespun was also used for aprons, underclothes, curtains, and bedding until the Revolution.

We have examples of linsey-woolsey bedcovers made by the German settlers in Pennsylvania. As was done in Europe, the weavers set up their looms with a homespun linen warp, and dyed their wool in indigo and red, and sometimes brown, for the weft. Since the looms set up in private homes were not large, two finished widths were sewn together down the center, or three widths were used if the spread was to fit a wide bed and extend to the floor. To make the spread, a piece of homespun linen or cotton was woven equal in size to the linsey-woolsey top, and the two were basted together with a thin pad of natural unwashed wool between. Then the whole was stretched over four stout sticks fashioned for the purpose. The design to be quilted was drawn on the front of the spread, and fine even stitches were used to catch and hold the three layers firmly together. The designs for quilting were many: baskets of flowers, leaves, ferns, feather wreaths, diagonal lines, basket weave, waffle, and pineapples. Usually, the main feature of the design was made to stand out in contrast with close background quilting in parallel diagonal lines or various sizes of crisscross lines. The edges of the finished coverlet were then turned in and sewn together, or bound with a contrasting hand-loomed tape.

Most of the linsey-woolsey spreads that have survived are indigo blue. This dark color did not show soil, and it was a color that held well. Lighter blues, often in an aqua tone are also seen, as well as shades of brown, red, deep blue-green, pink, and sometimes yellow. Shelburne Museum even has a linsey-woolsey spread that is pure white in color as well as one in a plaid design. The red "linseys" all seem quite similar as if they were made in one locality. The fabric and stitching used in this type are very coarse, the wool stuffing is thicker, and the shades of red are of many varieties, some very bright. These red spreads had a tendency to wear out, or wear through in spots, so the frugal housewife cut them into blocks and pieced them into bold designs of triangles or squares of two or three shades. The backs of these pieced linseys

19 (opposite). Pencil-post bed, with hangings of handloomed American silk made in Connecticut. The spread, also made of silk, is finely quilted in a large pattern (similar to a linsey-woolsey quilting design) of feather scrolls, with a central medallion and borders in a shell pattern. 105″ × 98″. The valence was reworked from an early, imported, silk-embroidered coverlet. (New Hampshire Historical Society)

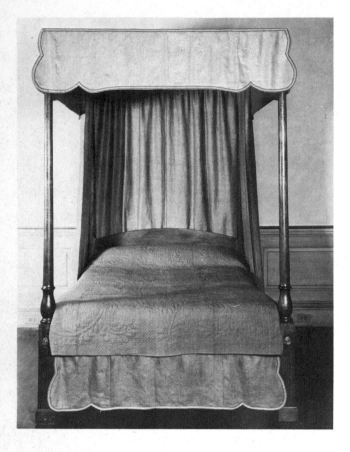

20 (above). Linsey-woolsey bedcover, 1775–1830, which is possibly English. 86½" × 81". The quilt is yellow-green and patterned with large foliate scrolls. (Winterthur Museum)

21 (opposite). Detail of a linsey-woolsey bedcover showing the sculpturesque effect created by the quilted design stuffed with a coarse wool filling. (Winterthur Museum)

are often a serge-weave homespun that was less time consuming than the usual homespun "tabby" weave. They were also quilted in white thread whereas the finest examples of linseys are sewn with matching thread.

The calimanco spread is very closely associated with linsey-woolsey. Today, if the weave of the fabric is fine, and there is a glow to the spread, it is called calimanco. This is not an altogether accurate term, since, strictly speaking, calimanco was a woolen fabric, similar to linsey-woolsey, imported from Flanders. It has a "checkered" warp, which shows only from the front, and it sometimes has a satin twill weave. Examples of true calimanco are seldom found today.

The spreads in our museums, sometimes labeled calimanco, were treated in several ways to achieve their satin gloss. Before it was quilted the fabric was most commonly rubbed with a smooth soft stone until it began to shine. Any man with a well-worn, blue-serge suit knows that wool shines when well rubbed. Also, the woolen fabric could be "glazed" (as chintz was being glazed in India and Europe) either with a mixture of egg white and water that was brushed on and allowed to dry and then polished, or with gum arabic or some other resinous substance.

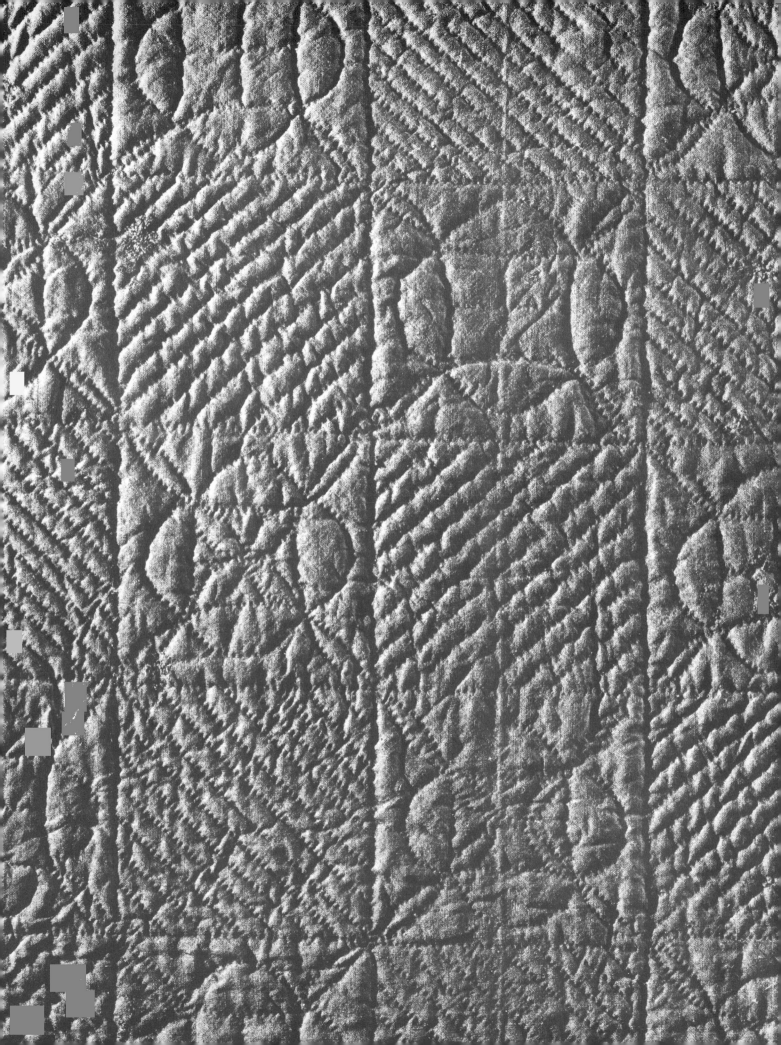

24 (right). Linsey-woolsey, c. 1785, New England 98″ × 98″. Faded olive-green wool with orangey-pink wool. The quilting is coarse, and the design includes seven hearts; so this may have been a marriage quilt. (Henry Ford Museum)

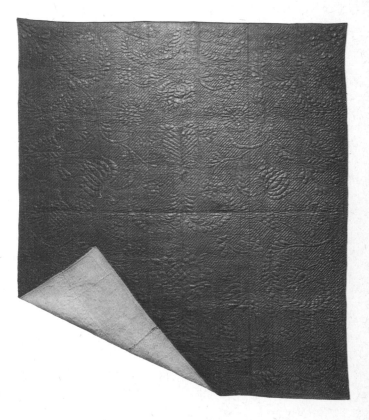

23 (left). Linsey-woolsey, c. 1790, American (?). Detail showing central design. 77″ × 75½″. This bright-red coverlet is very closely quilted in a series of circles, arcs, and rosettes in parallel lines. It is unlike any design on record. (Privately owned)

22 (opposite). A heavily glazed indigo-blue linsey-woolsey spread worked in an extremely large feather design. It combines beautifully with the blue-and-white resist-dyed hangings on a pencil-post bed in this bedroom of c. 1730 in the Prentis House. (Shelburne Museum, Inc.)

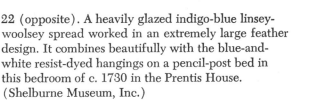

25 (right). Glazed linsey-woolsey, c. 1775, New England. 96″ × 84″. The brilliant "watermelon pink" of this "linsey" was not an unusual color at the time the spread was made, but note the striking yellow lining. The graceful irregularity of an India print has been worked into the quilting design. (Ginsburg & Levy, Inc.)

26 (above). Linsey-woolsey, 1750–1800, Windham, Vermont.
95″ × 92″. Made of butternut-dyed wool with a natural
linen back, and quilted in a very organized and unusual
combination of design elements. (Henry Ford Museum)

27 (opposite, left). Christening quilt, 1746, Philadelphia.
42″ × 42″. Quilted like a linsey, this piece is made of
white silk that has yellowed with age. Because of the delicacy
of the fabric, silk quilts did not weather the years as well as
wool, but a few examples do remain in good condition.
(San Antonio Museum Association)

28 (right), 28a (below, right). Glazed indigo linsey-woolsey, c. 1780, Connecticut. 92″ × 90″. The beautifully conceived and drawn design of this piece suggests that it was taken from a design book. The detail shown in figure 28a is from a light olive-green, twill-woven linsey-woolsey, c. 1775, very similar in pattern to figure 28. (Henry Ford Museum)

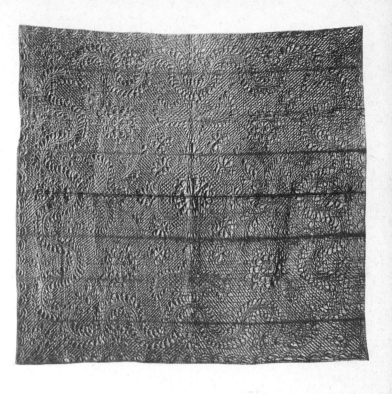

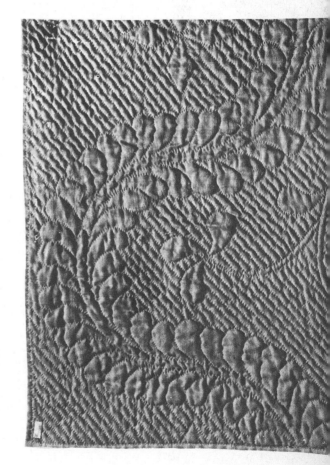

29 (left). Pieced linsey-woolsey, c. 1790, New York or Pennsylvania. 98½" × 93½". Alternating rows of beige and dark-blue diamonds are crisscrossed with bright-red stripes centered with light-blue squares. A design for using pieces saved from other linsey spreads, this example is more complicated than usual. (Privately owned)

30 (left). Pieced linsey-woolsey, c. 1785, Pennsylvania(?). 86" × 76½". The quilting pattern indicates that these linsey pieces were made (or saved) to be patched together into this design. (Privately owned)

31 (above), 31a (opposite, right). Glazed linsey-woolsey spread of a warm apricot color (actually, probably a quite faded pink) lined with olive-green wool, c. 1780, New York or New England. 95½″ × 92″. A unique and well-drawn design with a double feather border, grapes, floral sprays, and an impressively large heart! (Privately owned)

32 (above). Glazed linsey-woolsey, patchwork in an eight-pointed star design, c. 1800, New York or Pennsylvania. 93¼″ × 77½″. A deep watermelon pink combined with dark brown, and quilted in oblique lines to fill each square. The pink sections have been pieced many times. (Privately owned)

33 (above). Glazed linsey-woolsey, c. 1800, New York. 101″ × 99″. This is a handsomely executed patchwork and quilting pattern with a brown background and the star in dark green. The eight-pointed star in figures 32 and 33 was a favorite design motif for spreads, as can be seen in figures 106, 109, 386, and 437. (Ginsburg & Levy, Inc.)

34 (below). Calimanco in striped patchwork, c. 1785, New York or Pennsylvania. 96″ × 96″. An unusual use of three styles of fabric. The drops are deep wine-red wool and the top is made of even stripes of pink calimanco and a woven pink-and-gold, silk-and-wool combination. (Ginsburg & Levy, Inc.)

35 (above), 35a (opposite, above). Bedcover printed by John Hewson, cotton, late eighteenth century, Philadelphia. 106¼″ × 103¼″. Few examples of eighteenth-century fabrics printed in America can be positively identified as to their maker, but John Hewson's can. He came to America in 1773 with Benjamin Franklin's blessing, after an apprenticeship in England. Martha Washington ordered handkerchiefs from him for her husband, General George Washington. This spread is a superb example of an eighteenth-century American printed fabric. Two complete spreads are known (see figure 36), and some fragments of John Hewson's printed fabrics have been appliquéd onto other spreads (see figure 94). (Winterthur Museum)

36 (opposite, below). Bedcover, printed cotton, late eighteenth century, by John Hewson, Philadelphia. 105″ × 102¾″. This spread differs in several details from the Winterthur example which, on close inspection, contains seven more butterflies in the central panel! (Philadelphia Museum of Art)

THE WHOLE-CLOTH SPREAD

With the growth of both population and wealth in the New World, ships arriving in Boston and New York brought silks and damasks from France and Italy, brocades and velvets from Spain, and printed chintzes from England. The desire to have the printed fabrics that were fashionable in London became so great that the demand could not be satisfied. These India chintzes, originally brought in trade to London from India, were used for men's and women's clothing, draperies, and bedhangings. England soon began its own manufacture of the chintzes. Even the English manufacturers, however, could not supply the demand when America started using the fabrics, and Parliament was forced ·to limit exports of fabrics. Not many of these printed cottons remain. Scraps from worn clothing were cut out and appliquéd in later years to fine white spreads, and many such examples still exist and are illustrated later in this book. A palampore of fine printed cotton survives as a bedspread in the collection of the Henry Ford Museum (figure 42). Printed in a "Tree-of-Life" pattern in brilliant colorings, with some elements overpainted by hand with transparent dyes to increase the color range, this example is probably of English origin, but its design is obviously inspired by Indian work. The borders surrounding the central motif have been cut and pieced and reassembled to make a coverlet with a cut-out foot-piece and an "envelope" to hide the bolsters at the top. It seems apparent this coverlet was transformed from a wall hanging to a bedspread many years ago since the fringe is handmade and resembles an eighteenth-century style of trimming.

In Boston it became very fashionable to decorate one's town house with many bolts of the same fabric, which could be ordered directly from Europe. The restoration at Colonial Williamsburg in Virginia reflects this "high style," for one can see there window hangings, upholstery, and bed curtains all made from the same piece of cloth. In 1776 John Adams described in his diary the "rich beds with crimson damask curtains and counterpanes" found at the homes of friends in Boston.

Samuel Sewall, the famous diarist, also of Boston, ordered from London in 1720 "Curtains and Vallens for a Bed with Counterpane, Headcloth and Tester of good yellow waterd camlet with trimming well made. . . ." His bed was thus furnished in a fine satin-weave wool with braid sewn onto the face of the "vallens" to make a pattern. The words "counterpane" and "coverlid" (coverlet) appear to have been used synonymously. The word "counterpaine" is believed to be derived from "counterpoint," which was in common use in Mary Stuart's time. She became a very skillful needleworker while a prisoner of the English. When she made an article of clothing for warmth, she put two pieces of fabric together, inserted a filling, and stitched them together at important points called "quilt points" or "counterpoints."

Thus "quilting" became a common word in the history of the bedcover.

The mention of fabrics (usually in a variety of confusing spellings) and their uses is common in letters, diaries, and inventories of the eighteenth century. In 1739 the opulent Isaac Royall house in Medford, Massachusetts, sported a "Crimson Silk Damask Bed with Counterpin" . . . a "Blew Cheney Bed" . . . and a "Red Cheney Bed." According to eighteenth-century dictionaries, cheney (also spelled variously) was a smooth woolen fabric. Peter Faneuil, another famous Bostonian, possessed an array unmatched in his city in 1743: "1 Green Harateen Bed, Bedst. . . 2 GreenSilk Quilts, 1 Workt Fustian Bed . . ¾ lined with Green Damask . . . a Blew Silk Quilt." "Workt" usually indicated crewel embroidered on fustian made of cotton and linen. "Harateen" was also a fine woolen fabric, and silk quilts were made of natural woven silk, quilted in the same manner and with designs similar to those made by country women. Taffeta is the modern term for this type of silk. Several examples of these silk spreads have been preserved, but their condition is usually poor. A famous and beautiful coverlet exhibited for many years at Mount Vernon has been "retired" because of its deterioration. A jonquil-yellow spread can be seen in the Prentis bedroom at the New-York Historical Society, and a soft pink example is in the Prentis House at Shelburne Museum in Vermont.

In general, the use of the whole-cloth spread follows this chronology. The seventeenth-century fabrics most often used for bed hangings and coverlets were of wool: cheney, serge, say, camblet. Only slightly less popular were the English versions of Indian calico or chintz. By the middle of the eighteenth century, chintz had become supreme, followed by the lighter-weight wools and silks: camblet, harateen, mohair, shalloon, and moreen. After 1775 the fabric most often mentioned is harateen, with cheney second and chintz third. Actually, these fabrics have survived in such small amounts it is often impossible to distinguish between them, and dictionaries of the period are not sufficiently detailed to give real assistance. I often feel the difference lies mostly in the term in vogue, just as would be true today.

The eighteenth century also introduced copperplate printing and toiles. By the nineteenth century the copperplate had almost taken over completely, and chintz, as we know it today, was common. This was a big step in bedcoverings: fabric by the yard that could be purchased for making into coverlets at home—or by "your decorator."

Almost no examples of damask, brocade, or velvet spreads exist from this early period. Quilting helped preserve spreads made of satin and printed fabrics, but the heavy, rich fabrics were not quilted, so they wore out sooner and ended up as pieces in crazy quilts, two hundred years later. Our restorations of formal interiors, such as those at Winterthur and Williamsburg, often use spreads fashioned by modern upholsterers from period fabrics such as these.

37 (below). This illustration shows portions of curtains made of resist-dyed linen in two shades of blue on white, with a binding of printed tape specifically made to be sewn on as trimming. Hudson River Valley area, c. 1750. This type of trimming was often used for whole-cloth spreads bordered with fringes and braids. (Henry Ford Museum)

38 (opposite, above). Bedspread (palampore), India, 1700–1725, cotton twill. 102″ × 90″. The India-printed cotton was embellished with multicolored embroidery in a very fine chain stitch. (The Colonial Williamsburg Foundation)

39 (above, left), 39a (opposite, above right). Palampore, cotton, India or England, c. 1775. 91″ × 84″. Printed and painted by hand from wood blocks, this type of spread was uncommon and highly desired in fashionable homes. (Ginsburg & Levy, Inc.)

40 (above, right). Detail of a cotton bedspread made in India for the spice traders, 1775–1800. Dimensions of entire spread: 101½″ × 80″. Because the design is much less complicated, this spread was easier to print than the usual palampore, as seen in figures 38 and 39. (Winterthur Museum)

41 (below). Palampore, unlined and printed, English, c. 1800.
Reds and blues are the predominant colors. 116″ × 78″. The
extreme popularity of the decorated bedcover caused it to be copied
by English fabric printers, who made the designs a little lighter
and less complex than those made in India, and the subject
matter a little more Western. (Ginsburg & Levy, Inc.)

42 (right). Palampore, England (?), 1775–1800, printed cotton.
84″ × 47″, with drops on three sides. A magnificent example of a
printed and painted palampore made to fit a specific bed. In
so doing the basic "Tree of Life" structure of the design remains,
but the borders have been cut and pieced to make the spread
hang to the floor. The trimming and fringe are probably of a
somewhat later date. Lining also added. An unreadable stamp
on the fabric may indicate it was an East India import.
(Henry Ford Museum)

44 (right). Block-printed cotton coverlet, c. 1790, American (?), from Maine. 110″ × 106″. Quilted cotton printed in dark red-and-tan flowers in an all-over pattern. This large spread was made to fall to the floor. (Cincinnati Art Museum)

43, 43a (above). Block-printed quilted chintz coverlet, c. 1795, England. 94″ × 90″. A delightfully decorative spread with baskets of roses printed on a white ground. (Cora Ginsburg)

45 (below). Block-printed cotton coverlet, England or France, c. 1800. 102″ × 102″. A tightly designed repeat of exotic flowers and leaves in red, blue, green, and yellow with black outlines. This design shows a definite Eastern influence. (Henry Ford Museum)

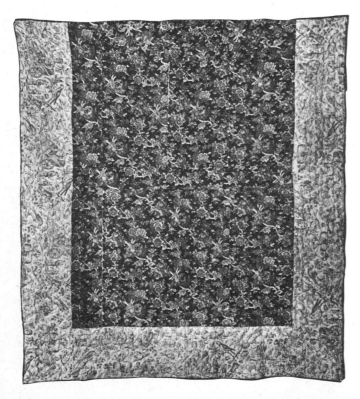

46 (above, left). Spread of quilted English chintz, c. 1830. 99″ × 81½″. This "pillar" or "column" chintz enjoyed a great popularity in America. Based on classic architectural detail, it has American roses and daisies. (Rhea Goodman: Quilt Gallery, Inc.)

47 (left). Lined, quilted spread combining India chintz and French toile de jouy, c. 1820, from Maine. 94″ × 84″. This spread also needed "piecing out." The center panel of floral chintz, dating c. 1780, is earlier than the spread. The background is very dark with red, blue, and tan exotic flowers. The border on three sides is made of blue toile of a later period. (Henry Ford Museum)

48 (center). Quilted spread of French toile de jouy lined in linen homespun, probably New England, c. 1785. 94″ × 72″. Piecing was necessary to make a spread large enough to use as a bedcover. The pattern of the toile is called "The Death of General Wolfe at the Battle of the Plains of Abraham." (Henry Ford Museum)

49 (below). Quilted spread of India-printed cotton, c. 1775, Boston. 93″ × 76″. This spread belonged to Mrs. John Hancock, wife of the Governor. The India silk lining is a soft yellow, and is equally as attractive as the rare imported print. (The Bostonian Society)

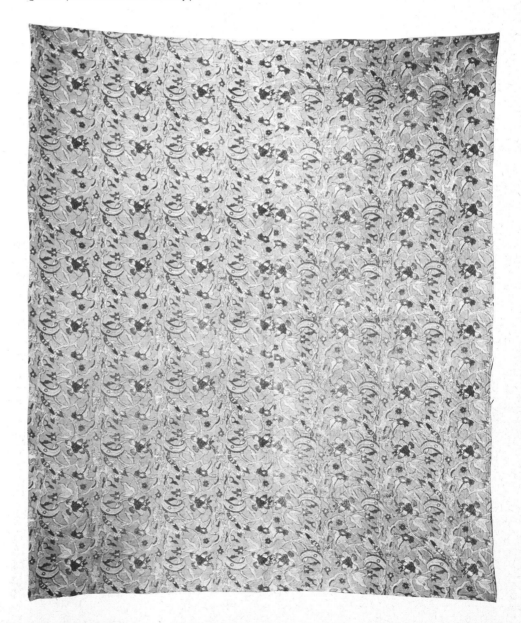

51 (left), 51 a (below). Bedcover made of resist-dyed fabric, a textile that is peculiarly American and generally from the Hudson River Valley area, c. 1775. 90″ × 80″. The pattern is large and in two shades of blue on white and the spread has been pieced together with no attempt to match the elements of the design. It is from the Frick family of Hoosick Falls, New York. (Ginsburg & Levy, Inc.)

50 (opposite). Detail of a coverlet of English toile, c. 1785. 90″ × 74″. Printed in England for export to America, this toile is a deep red. The pattern is known as "Apotheosis of Benjamin Franklin and George Washington." Many small fragments of this pattern exist. This large piece has remained intact since it was quilted to a back of linen homespun and made into a bedcover. (Winterthur Museum)

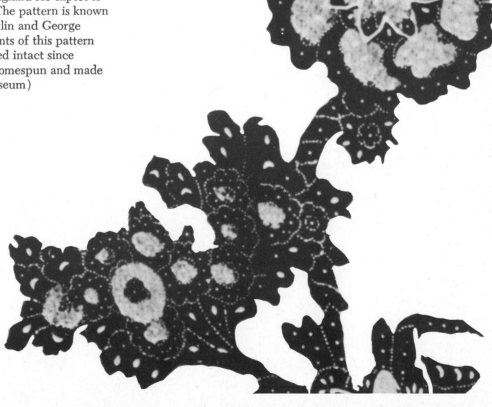

THE "WORKT" SPREAD

In the 1960s there was a tremendous resurgence of interest in the art of crewel embroidery. In this chapter we illustrate some eighteenth- and nineteenth-century examples of this particularly beautiful form of needlework that are distinctively American because of the naturalness and originality with which they have been designed and executed. In fact, the best examples of American crewel that remain to us were produced by women in small communities who had little or no access to English copybooks (i.e., design books), and thus depended on their own imaginative skills.

Ever since Jacobean times English crewel had generally been stiff in appearance and dark in color, with the ground completely stitched. Designs combined influences from Persia, India, and China with the English love for family crests, scrolls, and symbolic animals. English work was always surrounded with borders, or a series of borders in geometrics. The new American spirit found in New Hampshire, New York, New Jersey, and Virginia was loose and free, with no confining borders, and with open space around the motifs. Animals and people were drawn and shown as real: the parson, the bluebird, flowers growing in open fields. Thus the appeal of American crewel depends much on its naïve, untutored charm—its free spirit unfettered by pattern-book stiffness, taking its inspiration from many sources. Dutch women on Long Island and the Germans in Pennsylvania added tulip-like flowers. In New England, Maryland, and Virginia the feather crest of the Prince of Wales often became a framework for holding native flowers in line (more noticeable perhaps in the designs for "trapunto" to be discussed in the next chapter).

American crewel was embroidered on a not-too-fine linen homespun. Much of the linen produced by professional weavers in small towns was marked and sold to be "workt," that is "embroidered." A bit later, when wool became popular and a mark of wealth, "darnick" was woven in a soft satin finish also to be "workt." European "crewel" had been named for a town that produced the fine, loosely twisted wools in many colors. American women used whatever came to hand, including cotton and silk. Always self-reliant, they made their thread and invented their light and airy stitches—feather, seed, outline, French knot, etc. The earliest crewel we have was probably worked in blue, or various shades of blue, until the use of other colors developed from the discovery of the natural dyes that could be obtained from boiling herbs and barks in water.

More than half the examples of American crewel that now exist are borders—units of design in more or less straight horizontal lines. Understandably, a piece of crewel was cherished by its creator, and none was thrown away until it had seen its last bit of wear. Thus it was the valence that outlasted the other units of the bed dressing, and was tucked away in the attic. The counterpane was probably worn out and discarded first, being most handled, and so today we find many more sets of side and head curtains than coverlets. Fortunately, the crewel bed hangings make a perfect setting for linsey-woolsey and calimanco spreads; therefore the furnishing of a period bed is often done in this way, without the crewel spread.

Since American crewel embroidery developed in such diverse ways, our further discussion of coverlets is probably best understood from some individual examples. A rare spread (now in a private collection), made in 1749 and found in Rhinebeck, New York, was embroidered in blue on white linen. It is almost entirely covered with a pattern of lines that intertwine in three vertical columns to make irregular ovals filled with all manner of animal life. The design obviously developed as it was worked and is delightful for its lack of study and plan. Completely opposite in feeling is the crewel spread on a quarter-canopy bed in the Walnut Room at Winterthur Museum. It is worked on linen in blue, green, red, and yellow, but the method of balancing the units and the wide undulating border show the work of a real designer—a needlewoman who drew her pattern first, decided upon the placement of colors, and then proceeded to work it out in her favorite stitches. There is also a great deal more solid stitchery in this formal, more tutored example, which is probably of a slightly later period than the Rhinebeck spread, and perhaps more of a Southern adaptation.

Another crewel spread of the mid-eighteenth century is seen on a full canopy bed in the Cecil Bedroom at Winterthur (figures 58, 58a). Here the design was planned exactly to fill the top of the bedcover, and the "fall" at the foot becomes a very neat row of stylized flowers and leaves. An added feature not often seen in crewel work is the use of "strapwork" to add emphasis to the design and strengthen its form. The strapwork is made of "coach" braid or an imported trimming such as was used in Europe on clerical robes. This important spread was made for a Boston shipper and then inherited by his nephew, John Hancock (of the famous signature on the Declaration of Independence).

52 (opposite). Bed completely hung with crewel work on a linen homespun. It was made c. 1745 by one person, Mary Bulman, wife of Dr. Alexander Bulman of York, Maine. (Old Gaol Museum)

I'LL CARUE OUR PASSION ON THE BARK
AND EUERY WOUNDED TREE
SHALL DROP AND BEAR SOME MYSTIC MARK
THAT IESUS DY'D FOR ME

Embroidery on wool became popular about 1850 and continued through the Victorian period. Strictly speaking, this is not crewel work, but simply embroidery, with fewer types of stitches used and a general coarsening of effect. The wool background was usually a homespun woven in two widths and sewn together down the middle. Many examples of simple checks were woven and embellished with a geometrical-type flower or leaf. These are often merely called "blankets" in the old inventories, and most of these have New York or Pennsylvania histories. The Henry Ford Museum has a large spread in a twill-weave woolen embroidered with large flowers, leaves, and scrolls, but using just one embroidery stitch (figure 71). The Witte Memorial Museum in San Antonio, Texas, has a similar spread with hand-knotted edging that makes it very rare example (figure 80).

Several examples of coverlets exist that have dark woolen backgrounds. They are quite Victorian in their design, and brilliant and jewel-like in color. The use of urns of flowers to fill the whole spread is typical of these pieces.

THE SWAINS SHALL WONDER WHEN THEY READ
INSCRIB'D ON ALL THE GROVE
THAT HEAVEN ITSELF CAME DOWN AND BLED
TO WIN A MORTALS LOVE

52a (above), 52b (center), 52c (opposite, below), 52d below). Crewel-worked valence and spread, c. 1745, made by Mary Bulman. Dimensions of spread, 79″ × 73½″. No record to the contrary, it is believed that Mary Bulman designed and executed herself all the parts of this massive work to "occupy her mind" while her husband was serving as a surgeon under Sir William Pepperrell at the Siege of Louisburg. He died at Cape Breton in 1745. The verses testify to her loneliness. They are taken from the poem "Meditation in a Grove" in *Horae Lyricae* by Isaac Watts, 1706. (Old Gaol Museum)

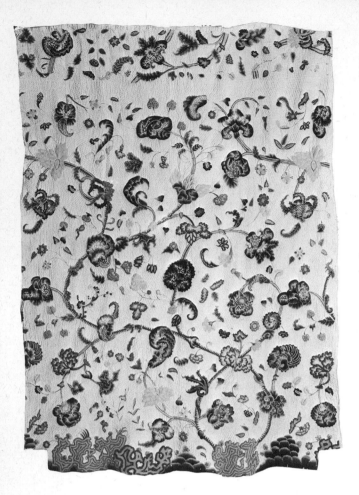

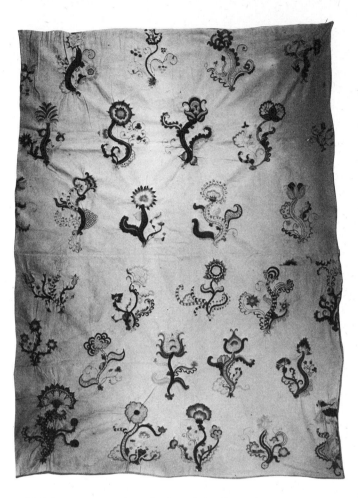

53 (left). Embroidered quilt, Boston, 1711–14, made by Mary Thurston Fifield and her daughter, Mary. 78¾″ × 56″. Cotton with linen warp, twill woven, crewel embroidered in many colors and stitches. This spread resembles English examples and was probably part of a complete set of bed hangings. (Museum of Fine Arts, Boston)

55 (above). Crewel-worked coverlet, linen homespun, c. 1750, Montville, Connecticut. 80″ × 54″. Multicolored sprays of flowers worked in several crewel stitches. Note the mermaid (!) peeking from beneath the flower in the bottom row. An outstanding example of typical New England crewel. (The New-York Historical Society)

54 (left). Crewel coverlet, cotton and linen ground, c. 1730, New York. 101″ × 98″. Many-colored and richly stitched in solids, this is a remarkable piece of American crewel. Twenty years in the making (1728–1748), it was created by Clarissa Stohard who married Moses Seyo on April 7, 1728, and lived in Springtown near New Paltz, New York. (The Colonial Williamsburg Foundation)

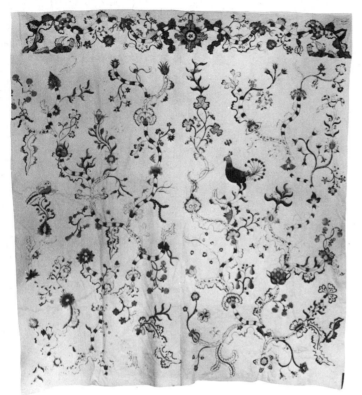

56 (above, left), 56a (above, right). Polychrome crewel coverlet made by Prudence (Geer) Punderson of Preston, Connecticut, late eighteenth century. 81″ × 55″. As preserved, this coverlet is made of two bed curtains in polychrome crewel sewn together with a section of what was originally a valence added at the top. When used on a bed, the valence portion of this spread would act as a drop over the foot of the bed. (The Connecticut Historical Society)

57 (right). This embroidered self-portrait is a detail taken from the famous "Mortality Picture" made between 1776 and 1783 by Prudence (Punderson) Rossiter, daughter of the Prudence Punderson who worked the crewel spread illustrated above. She is seen seated at her "designing board," working perhaps on one of her extraordinary series of needlework portraits of the "Twelve Apostles," in which they are depicted as Puritan divines. (The Connecticut Historical Society)

58 (above), 58a (left). Crewel-embroidered coverlet, part of a complete set of bed hangings on linen, c. 1750, provenance unknown. 112″ × 78½″. This is a very unusual combination of applied strapwork and floral designs in shades of rose, blue, green, and yellow. These bed furnishings were originally owned by Thomas Hancock, a Boston merchant and ship owner, and later by his nephew, John Hancock. (Winterthur Museum)

60 (right). Crewel coverlet, c. 1740, made by Sarah Noyes Chester of Wethersfield, Connecticut. 88" × 70½". Embroidered on linen homespun in rose, yellow, green, tan, and cream wools. Satin, split, stem, star, and French knot stitches are used together with block shading and cross-stitch filling. One of Sarah Chester's daughters married Joseph Webb, and the remainder of the bed set is in the Webb House in Wethersfield. (The Metropolitan Museum of Art, Gift of Mr. and Mrs. Frank Coit Johnson through their son and daughter, 1944)

59 (above). Crewel bedspread, dated 1770, made by Mary Breed of Boston. 94½" × 87½". Embroidered in wool in shades of pink, yellow, blue, and green. Several stitches are used, but Roumanian stitch predominates. The cutting of the foot corners was evidently done for a second bed, since the embroidery has obviously been cut into. (The Metropolitan Museum of Art, Rogers Fund, 1922)

61 (right). Crewel spread, c. 1740, Massachusetts. 87" × 72". A very linear design created by long sweeps of vines and scrolls. The top (or center section) of this linen homespun is woven in a diaper pattern and is in excellent condition. The drops are in the usual linen homespun and show more deterioration. (Henry Ford Museum)

62 (left), 62a (opposite). Coverlet of white cotton twill signed and dated "Judith Smith, 1790," Virginia. 83″ × 72″. Completely embroidered in white cotton in a variety of stitches, it consists of three narrow widths sewn together. The design is completely original and neatly arranged. (Valentine Museum)

63 (left), 63a (above). Linen coverlet embroidered in blue crewel, c. 1800, New York or New England. 90″ × 80″. There are several crewel-work stitches used in this delightfully original coverlet, although it seems at first glance to be quite linear in feeling. The drawing of the design is obviously freehand, as we can see by the handling of the usually troublesome corners. (Cora Ginsburg)

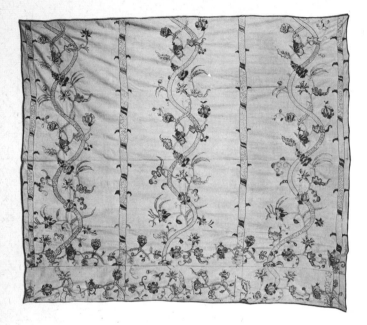

64 (left), 64a (above). Crewel-embroidered bedspread and valence, c. 1750. 98″ × 84″. The intertwining flower and vine pattern in three panels is done in blues, pinks, greens, tan, and lavender wool on white homespun. Both the valence and spread are bound in a hand-loomed tape. The valence is worked in a familiar design, but the spread shows an appealing originality. (The New-York Historical Society)

65 (right), 65a (above). Silk bedcover of a deep plum color, embroidered in polychrome silks, c. 1780, China. 114″ × 114″. A sumptuous spread, extraordinarily complex in design, of a type imported for use in the wealthiest American homes of the period. (Ginsburg & Levy, Inc.)

66 (above). Silk bedcover, c. 1780, China. 98″ × 69″. Another resplendent coverlet
with polychrome embroidery rather similar to Western crewel. (Ginsburg & Levy, Inc.)

67 (above). Wool bedcover embroidered by Harriet
Dumbar, c. 1760. 90″ × 88″. Polychrome crewel wools in
several stitches are used in this design on black twilled wool.
(Wadsworth Atheneum)

68 (below). Embroidered bedcover in black wool, c. 1770.
96″ × 80″. The all-over floral design is enchanting.
(Henry Ford Museum)

69 (above). Embroidered wool coverlet, late eighteenth century, New England. 100″ × 94″. Black twill, handwoven in 32″ widths, embroidered in beiges and greens. The fringe is green wool. (The Colonial Williamsburg Foundation)

70 (below), 70a (above). Wool coverlet made by Premella Goodall, Buffalo, c. 1790. 98½″ × 88″. Three widths of wool homespun, with needlework in shades of blue and gold wool. The designs are delightfully original in conception. (Henry Ford Museum)

71 (center): Wool coverlet, initialed and dated "A L 1832." 82″ × 72″. Embroidered in red and blue, and using only one crewel stitch. (Henry Ford Museum)

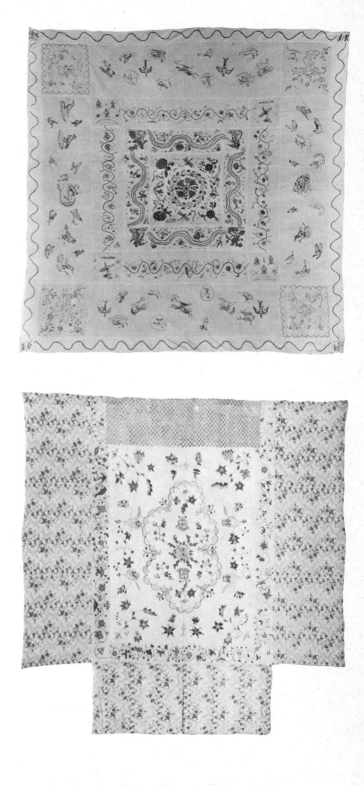

72 (above). Linen homespun coverlet, signed and dated "Annis Clark, aged 13, November 24, 1818." 108″ × 108″. A home-designed cover using birds for the main theme. The work is almost completely linear. (Ginsburg & Levy, Inc.)

73 (below). Coverlet, crewel work on linen, c. 1760. 96½″ × 94″. The small groups of flowers are typically American in style. The drops are of printed cotton and quilted. (Cincinnati Art Museum)

74 (above), 74a, 74b, 74c, 74d (left), 74e (below). Wool bedcover, 1778, New York. 96½" × 76½". Cream-colored homespun wool blanket, with squares embroidered in indigo blue and filled with designs suggesting Delft tiles. Patterns are flowers, leaves, birds, and grapes, among others. Some of the stitches are similar to formal crewelwork, others are very naïve. Inscribed "S(?) M D. A L. 78." The spread shows a strong Dutch influence and may well have been made by a Dutch-born woman living in New York. Blue fringe on three sides. (Henry Ford Museum)

75 (above). Embroidered, handwoven blanket, signed and dated "Caroline M. Sloane,
Stockbridge, 1853." 86″ × 78″. The blanket is woven in a check pattern with red
and blue in the warp and weft. The embroidery is done in two designs of floral sprays,
one heavily solid, and one light. (Ginsburg & Levy, Inc.)

76, 76a, 76b, 76c (below), 76d (opposite). Wool bedcover, 1810–1840. 117″ × 92″. Quilted bedcover with patchwork of wool applied in a diamond checkerboard pattern, and embroidered in polychrome wools. The designs are more reminiscent of a quilt pattern than crewel. Patchwork colors are plum, brown, blue, and black. (Winterthur Museum)

77 (right). Wool bedcover, 1800–1820. 105½″ × 102″. Quilted wool bedcover with plain, woven wool appliquéd in strips and embroidered in crewel. Many stitches—outline, flat, cross, seed, satin, and buttonhole—are used. Designs are not typical early crewel patterns. (Winterthur Museum)

78 (left). Embroidered check blanket, signed and dated "Catherine Johnson The 1846." 94″ × 78½″. Embroidery is in black wool, suggesting tile, with a floral border as contrast. Applied white fringe. (Privately owned)

79 (below, left). Check blanket embroidered in blue, c. 1850. 98″ × 75″. The design is very similar to the example above. Photograph courtesy Ginsburg & Levy, Inc. (Genesee Country Museum)

80 (below). Embroidered cotton bedcover, c. 1820, American (?). 94″ × 74″. Crewel-work in rose, pink, dark and light blue, and yellow. Stylized flowers and leaves are typical crewel designs of the period, few stitches being used. The macramé edging is outstanding. Although purchased in Mexico, it bears more resemblance to work being done in New York State at the time. (San Antonio Museum Association)

"WHITE WORK"

Another very popular type of eighteenth-century needle-work is "white work," also a form of quilting. Commonly called "trapunto," it is thought to have come from Italy to England about the time of Queen Anne. From England it spread to the Colonies, especially in the cities and the South. Trapunto comprises two fabrics quilted together with no stuffing between. The top fabric was always a fine white cotton; the bottom a linen or cotton homespun. After these two fabrics were sewn together in an intricate design of extremely fine stitches, the individual parts of the design were stuffed with soft cotton from the back through the loosely woven homespun. Every part of the design was filled in this way, producing a sculptured effect with highlights and shadows. The scarcity of cotton suitable for this delicate work made trapunto rather rare, but, being made of cotton, examples of this work have usually survived in better condition than spreads of wool or silk.

Trapunto was popular in the Northern Colonies at the same time as linsey-woolsey coverlets, and it shared many of the same design elements, such as feather wreaths, prince's plumes, roping, cornucopias, baskets of flowers, and leaves. Designs in trapunto work could show much more detail, and diagonal parallel lines in great numbers filled the areas between designs. Since the stitches in trapunto were much more noticeable if they were not extremely small and precise, no needleworker started a white-work spread until she was sure of her patience

81 (above), 81a (opposite), 81b (below). Trapunto coverlet, c. 1810. 95" × 85". The fine draftsmanship in this example of a "white work" spread is apparent. There is perfect balance of forms, and beautiful contrast in the delicacy and strength of the component parts. This piece was probably created as a wedding quilt. (Rhea Goodman: Quilt Gallery, Inc.)

and proficiency. Such needlework was unquestionably her final test of craftsmanship, especially because it was white. We are fortunate that many unbelievably fine examples survive in mint condition in various public and private collections. The same precise workmanship was required in the early appliqué quilts, and they also represent one of the finest products of our early American homes.

It should be noted that when a piece of trapunto pears to be made of linen, instead of cotton, is coarser, and the design consists of lines (parallel, concentric, diagonal, etc.) more than of pictorial designs it is probably Sicilian cable work. This style of quilting was popular at the same time as white work, but it was chiefly made in communities of Italian immigrants. Cording was inserted between the top and bottom layers of fabric to emphasize the design.

A particularly famous trapunto spread is a very late example, called the "Secession Quilt," made in 1860. It is one of a pair of quilts made by a Mrs. Cook, the wife of a general of the South Carolina militia, for her grand-daughters; and her needlework designs mirror the South's strong feelings for Secession. Mrs. Cook raised cotton herself, but chose to use it only for the stuffing of the designs since her woven cotton was not fine enough to use for the fabric of the spread. A finer, imported grade of cotton was bought for this purpose. The designs were drawn with exquisite care after a plan that required real artistic talent. There are fruits, garlands of flowers, and four repeats of the arms of the state of South Carolina. Above these arms are the names of four governors during the years from 1830 to 1838, all champions of the South. Washington's name appears in the center of the quilt near the representation of Liberty; and "E Pluribus Unum" is written on a banner held in the beak of an eagle with outstretched wings. Obviously, Mrs. Cook had faith in her country, her state, and her patience! One of these quilts was destroyed by Union soldiers who cut it into saddlecloths, but the other remains as an unbelievable work of art. It was illustrated and described in the February 1929 issue of The Magazine *Antiques*, and it is probably still in a private collection.

The crib coverlet shown in figure 83 is almost the peer of the Secession Quilt. It has no patriotic background, but its exquisite detail and handmade tassel fringe show more than any words its maker's love for her child. It must be seen to be believed.

In this form of needlework where both draftsmanship and craftsmanship had to be so exacting, the designs are usually very carefully worked out. Very few of these white-work quilts show the use of transfer designs, but use instead the inventiveness of handed-down patterns. Backgrounds utilized basket weaves, crossbars, large and small diamonds, and splint (as seen in 1750 chair seats). The Oriental Tree-of-Life motif came to look more and more like a weeping willow. The pineapple became a symbol of hospitality, adapted from the Orient. The acanthus leaf was borrowed from a favorite type of architectural detailing, and waved lines were adapted from the Atlantic tides. Other design motifs were: the dove of peace that came to represent a social tea; the feather ring derived from the plume worn by women as a formal headdress; the oak leaf that symbolized strength and virility; and the pine tree that epitomized the spirit of America

82 (below). Detail from a stuffed-work bedcover, c. 1820. A very crisp effect is achieved by the regularity of the parts of the design—stems, leaves, basket reeding, etc. (New Hampshire Historical Society)

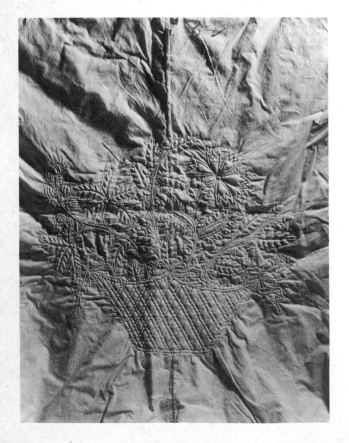

83 (opposite) Trapunto crib coverlet, c. 1820, New England. 60″ × 32″. The quality of the workmanship in this small masterpiece is staggering. It must have been the worshipful hands of a mother or grandmother that created such a gift of devotion to a child. The design is classical in its balance, using flowers, vases, leaves, stars, and (of course!) a heart. (Henry Ford Museum)

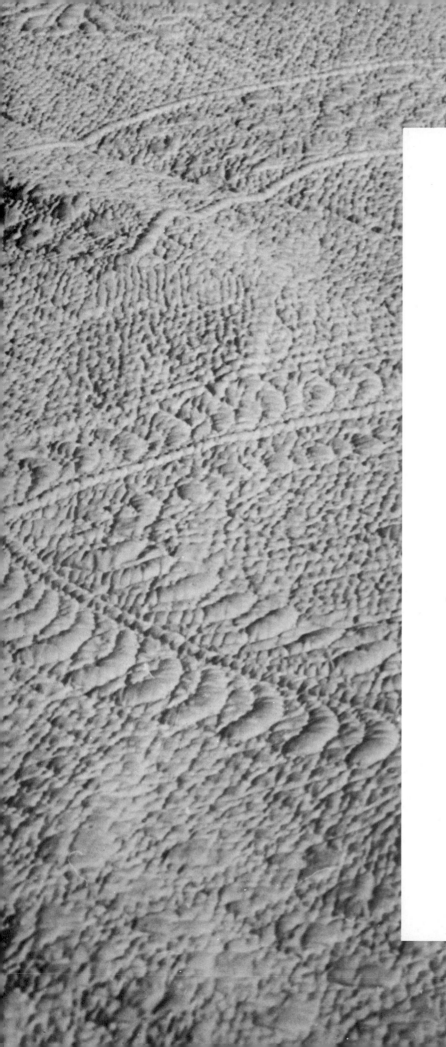

84 (below). Trapunto pillow sham, cotton, c. 1825, Pennsylvania (?). Handwoven cotton is the base for this set of bedcoverings. The design of feather wreath and undulating feather border is in bold relief against the background of diamond crisscross. (Old Economy Village)

85 (background). Detail of trapunto spread, cotton,
c. 1825, Pennsylvania (?). 103″ × 101″. The spread has
designs of grapes and vines, flowers with swirling
petals, and feather borders in many shapes.
(Old Economy Village)

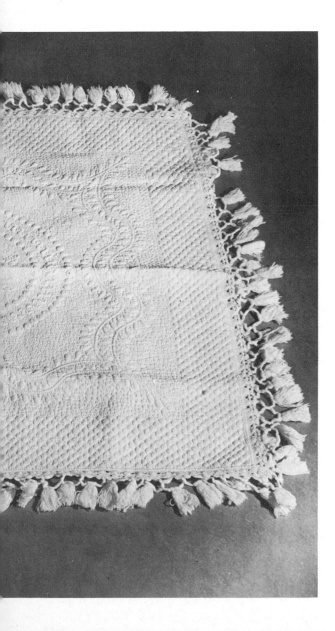

86 (above), 86a (left). Trapunto coverlet, cotton, inscribed "Ada Chew," c. 1820. 87¼" × 84¼". The contrast between the raised design and the minute work of the background makes this a unique piece of needlework. The spread is balanced to face four ways, and it features the pineapple, symbol of hospitality. (Privately owned)

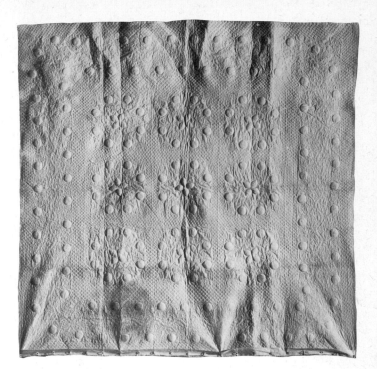

87 (right). Trapunto coverlet, cotton, c. 1845. 98″ × 83″. The design of this piece has a simple regularity, the groups of "snowballs" contrasting with the diagonal waffle ground. (Henry Ford Museum)

88 (below). Detail of a trapunto cradle coverlet, c. 1850. 43″ × 34″. Much of this minute, complicated design is in lines, and the stuffing could be "run in" with a blunt needle. The structure of this pattern is reminiscent of Renaissance work. (Privately owned)

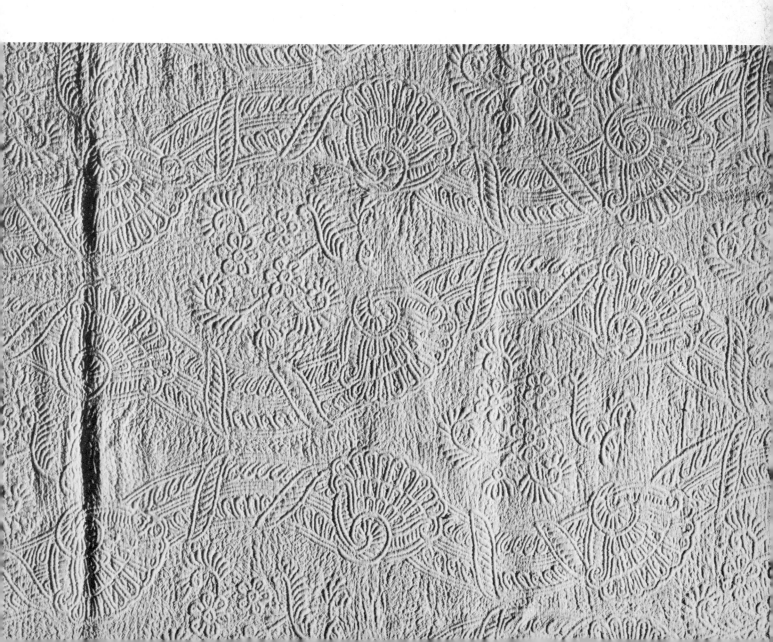

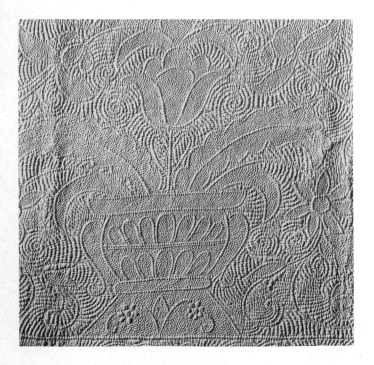

89 (above). Trapunto coverlet, cotton, c. 1820, New England.
77″ × 72″. Designed entirely with feather motifs contrasting
with a background worked in diagonal parallel lines going
in one direction. (Henry Ford Museum)

90 (left). Detail of a trapunto crib coverlet, cotton, c. 1840,
American (?). 65″ × 59″. Several examples of this extremely
fine stuffed work have been preserved. It resembles
Sicilian cable work and would probably have been made
in America. There is enough of parallel-line construction in
this piece to raise a question as to its provenance.
The design of flowers in a vase is very similar to a popular
Pennsylvania motif. (Good & Hutchinson Associates)

92, 92a (below). Trapunto coverlet, cotton, c. 1816, made by Lucy Foot of Colchester, Connecticut. 90″ × 87¾″. This coverlet was part of Lucy Foot Bradford's wedding outfit. An unusually strong design for stuffed work with handsome balance of design and beautiful execution. (The Stamford Historical Society, Inc.)

91 (center). Trapunto coverlet, cotton, dated 1838, made by Mary Anne Phares of Tennessee. 88″ × 84″. This coverlet has won several blue ribbons in Tennessee for being the oldest and best preserved quilt in the state. In the center of the star is a ring circling the inscription "M A P 1838," hence it was part of Mary Anne's bridal preparations. The design is bold and simple and the background areas have been left unworked. The family was of French Huguenot descent. (Ladies' Hermitage Association)

93 (above). Trapunto bedcover, cotton, c. 1893. 68″ × 66″. An intricate and well-drawn design based entirely on the plume or feather motif. The background of diagonal crisscrossing lines pushes the design into high relief. The scalloped border enhances the bold simplicity of the design. It was made prior to 1893, for it won a First Prize at the Chicago World's Fair in 1893. (San Antonio Museum Assocation)

94 (right), Trapunto and appliqué coverlet, cotton, c. 1807. 116⅓″ × 112¼″. This coverlet beautifully combines fine stuffed work with design elements cut from a spread printed by John Hewson of Philadelphia (see figures 35 and 36). Parts of the Hewson spread have been appliquéd onto the center of the piece with an undulating band of feather work added. This section is surrounded by a printed cotton border, which is in turn encircled by a "necklace" of trapunto. Then another border of printed cotton, and finally a wide trapunto border of vines and flowers. A masterful creation! (St. Louis Art Museum, Gift of Miss Mildred Petrie)

THE PATCHWORK QUILT

We are all familiar with patchwork quilts, for many of us have inherited them, or seen them in museums or antique shops. These quilts are fascinating not only for their marvelous variety of color and design, but also for their astonishing craftsmanship. We can only wonder at the sheer doggedness of the women who found joy in creating a work of art by cutting leftover pieces of fabric into one-inch squares, diamonds, or hexagons and then sewing them together again into a large, overall design.

In these geometrical creations every seam was a straight line. Any person who could thread a needle and sew could learn to make an even stitch in a straight line. In this way she assembled her countless dozens of pre-cut pieces; indeed, some pieced quilts have been counted, and contain over 4,000 patches.

The art of patchwork quilting flourished in the period 1775–1875, and the designs (and especially the naming of the designs) were inspired by many events, such as the admission of new states, the opening of the West, the railroad, and many political and social movements. New patterns developed largely in the rural areas, sometimes as a design that was entirely new, but usually they would be variations on patterns that had been traded between the womenfolk. The fabrics that were available in the country towns had a way of creating their own patterns!

Quilts came to be made in great numbers not principally as bedcovers, but as blankets for additional warmth. Tradition says that a chest filled with thirteen quilts was the goal of every young woman. When she was old enough to be taught to sew, the girl made a plain quilt. In succeeding steps she learned the complications of cutting, piecing, designing, and quilting. Her last quilt was the most ambitious in design. This she did not quilt herself; it became the "Bride's Quilt" and her friends were invited to spend the day at a "quilting bee" (see figure 95) to enjoy each other's company and help quilt the spread. The young men would join the women in the evening, and thus made a real social event of the occasion. A quilt survives that has embroidered on it the following admonition to other young women:

> At your quilting, maids don't dally,
> A maid who is quiltless at twenty-one,
> Never shall greet her bridal sun!

We are fortunate in that many splendid collections of quilts are found today all over America; fine examples are treasured in many museums and historical societies. As antiquarians, we study these quilts for their beauty of design and craftsmanship and for the variety of fabrics used in the individual patches—printed or plain, hand-

95 (above). *The Quilting Party*, artist unknown, third quarter of the nineteenth century. 13¼″ × 25¼″. This charming American folk painting perfectly captures the spirit of a household entertaining neighbors during a quilting bee. (Abby Aldrich Rockefeller Folk Art Collection)

woven or machine made. We especially value any specific documentation that is available for a quilt: the date it was made, for whom, when, and where.

Marguerite Ickis, a devoted student of patchwork quilting, provides a particularly touching example of personal documentation in the following quote from her great-grandmother who lived in Ohio:

> It took me more than twenty years, nearly twenty-five, I reckon, in the evening after supper when the children were all put to bed. My whole life is in that quilt. It scares me sometimes when I look at it. All my joys and all my sorrows are stitched into those little pieces. When I was proud of the boys and when I was down-right provoked and angry with them. When the girls annoyed me or when they gave me a warm feeling around my heart. And John too. He was stitched into that quilt and all the thirty years we were married. Sometimes I loved him and sometimes I sat there hating him as I pieced the patches together. So they are all in that quilt, my hopes, and fears, my joys and sorrows, my loves and hates. I tremble sometimes when I remember what that quilt knows about me.

The matter of size is worth special mention, for the size of a spread is so often a part of its story. Many quilts were obviously designed for individual beds, some to cover mountainous featherbeds, some to have flounces to the floor, some for beds built into the wall as in the Dutch-style houses. Over the years, beds grew smaller

and narrower, becoming by 1850 more or less standardized to our so-called antique three-quarter-size bed. The South enjoyed large beds, and most stood high off of the floor so as to be cooler. Quilts that were stored as extras to use on a cold night were not made to be tucked in but to be used as throws.

Finally, the finest spreads that have survived to the present time were the "best spreads" of their day: the best fabrics were saved for them, the most elaborate work was put into them, and they were preserved by using them only infrequently in a darkened guest room!

96, 97 (above, left), 98 (below, left), 99 (opposite), 99a (above). Patchwork quilt with matching pillows (17″ square) and sham (48″ × 25″), Sunburst or Rising Sun pattern, c. 1800, Maryland. 94″ × 72″. Many plain and printed cotton fabrics were used in this group. Each unit of the design is surrounded by a quilted feather circle, and the spaces between the circles are filled with waffle quilting. (Baltimore County Historical Society, Inc.)

100 (above). Detail of patchwork quilt, Star of Bethlehem, silk, c. 1835. The field of the star is light-blue silk, quilted in detail. (Philadelphia Museum of Art)

102 (center). Patchwork quilt, Rising Star, c. 1820. 104″ × 104″. Small diamonds in graded colors are used to make up the unusual four-petaled form. Chintz appliqué supplements the patchwork. (Privately owned)

101 (left). Detail of patchwork quilt, Star of Bethlehem, c. 1850. Patched with plain and printed cottons in several colors, the design is supplemented with fine quilting. (Philadelphia Museum of Art)

103 (above, right). Patchwork quilt, Star of Bethlehem, c. 1840, Pennsylvania (?). 85½″ × 82½″. Executed in "planned-color" combinations, this becomes a striking color creation. Corners are well filled with four miniature eight-pointed stars. (Privately owned)

104 (below, right). Patchwork and appliqué quilt top, Star of Bethlehem and Oakleaf, c. 1835, Pennsylvania (?). 87¼″ × 78¼″. The four corner designs start as eight-pointed stars but are filled so as to become almost circular. The appliqué units almost overfill the remaining spaces. The boldness of the color and the design give this piece a folk-art quality. Photograph courtesy Allan L. Daniel. (Rhea Goodman: Quilt Gallery, Inc.)

106 (above). Patchwork quilt, Feathered Star with Flying Geese borders between the blocks, c. 1835. 80½" × 71". A strong, handsome design. (Rhea Goodman: Quilt Gallery, Inc.)

107 (above). Patchwork quilt, Le Moyne Star or Lemon Star with octagonal center, c. 1860. 74" × 74". Made of drab prints and stripes of late date, against white. (Henry Ford Museum)

108 (above). Patchwork quilt, Sawtooth Star, c. 1876, Fowlersville, Michigan. 77" × 62". Elaborate quilting is an excellent foil for the sawtooth triangles in red, all set against white. (Henry Ford Museum)

111 (below). Patchwork quilt, Star of the East, c. 1840. 84" × 66". Worked in a red, white, and blue color scheme with small patriotic textile prints. (Henry Ford Museum)

109 (above). Patchwork quilt, Octagonal Star, c. 1840. 64" × 58". A complicated yet effective creation, especially in this red-and-blue combination. (Rhea Goodman: Quilt Gallery, Inc.)

110 (below). Imitation patchwork quilt, Kansas Star, c. 1860. 87" × 85". This coverlet is made of a printed fabric in red, yellow, and green that has been quilted. (George Schoellkopf: The Peaceable Kingdom, Ltd.)

112 (above). Patchwork quilt, Feathered Star, c. 1835. 86" × 85". The fine all-over quilting and the two sawtooth borders create a delicate effect in the red-on-white colors. (Henry Ford Museum)

113 (opposite, above). Patchwork quilt, Star of Bethlehem, c. 1835. 88½" × 86½". Blue ground, with red, pink, yellow, gray, and white in the star creating quite a dramatic effect. (Rhea Goodman: Quilt Gallery, Inc.)

114 (below). Patchwork quilt, Feathered Star, c. 1830. 92½″ × 82½″. Fine cross-hatch quilting covers this red-and-white quilt and combines effectively with undulating feather quilting and a large sawtooth border. (Rhea Goodman: Quilt Gallery, Inc.)

115 (above). Patchwork quilt, Star of Bethlehem (variation), c. 1934. 84″ × 84″. A unique variation on the Star design combined with feather and waffle quilting. (Henry Ford Museum)

116 (above). Patchwork quilt, Sunburst, c. 1840. 78¼" × 69½". An exciting, colorful effect created with fabrics that are mostly printed. (Rhea Goodman: Quilt Gallery, Inc.)

117 (left). Patchwork quilt, Star of Bethlehem, c. 1830. 123½″ × 105″. The foreshortening of the points of the star at the top is unusual. The background of this quilt is glazed chintz. (Philadelphia Museum of Art)

118 (below). Detail of a patchwork quilt, true Sunburst, c. 1840. 90″ × 84″. Nearly all the patches are made from printed fabric. (Henry Ford Museum)

119 (left). Patchwork quilt, Star of Bethlehem, c. 1830. 75½″ × 75¼″. The color in the blocks has been handled in such a way that circles rather than stars stand out in this red, pink, yellow, and white creation. The circles of feather quilting and undulating feather border add a masterful touch. (Privately owned)

120 (below). Patchwork and appliqué quilt, Star of Bethlehem (variation), c. 1830. 111¼″ × 110¼″. Because of the huge size of this spread, it is not shown in its entirety. A strongly designed and beautifully executed spread in brilliant blues and oranges. (Privately owned)

121 (below), 121a (right). Patchwork and appliqué quilt, Star of Bethlehem, c. 1845. 87″ × 85″. This striking red-on-white quilt gives the impression of being both simple and complex. The five small stars in the corners and the four eagles tend to unbalance the design. (Privately owned)

122 (above), 122a (above, right). Patchwork and appliqué quilt with embroidery, Le Moyne Star, c. 1825. Dimensions unavailable. The colors of this extraordinary "Kentucky Coffin Quilt" are tans, browns, and white. The outer border is a picket fence with some embroidered flowers growing between the pickets. Just inside the fence, coffins have been appliquéd and stitched with the name of each member of the family. As each member died, his casket would be permanently moved to the cemetery in the center of the quilt, where weeping willows can be seen. O tempora! O mores! (Kentucky Historical Society)

123 (left). Patchwork and appliqué quilt, Mariner's Compass, c. 1825. 93½″ × 92″. The magnificent compasses were cut from a red printed fabric, as were the appliquéd wreaths. This is probably the most difficult pattern in the patchwork quilt repertory because of the extreme narrowness and sharpness of the compass points. (Privately owned)

124 (above). Patchwork quilt, Feathered Star with Blazing Sun center, c. 1840. 91″ × 84″. An intricate pattern extremely well handled by an expert in sewing, who was also expert in the successful juxtaposition of unusual colors. (Rhea Goodman: Quilt Gallery, Inc.)

125 (left). Patchwork quilt, Star of the East, c. 1830, Ephrata, Pennsylvania, 101″ × 101″. The corners created by the central star are filled with Rising Suns also made of diamond patches. There is feather quilting in both circle and undulating designs. (Privately owned)

126 (below, left). Patchwork quilt, Star of the East, c. 1830. 82″ × 80″. The star enclosed in an octagon creates a striking effect. (Privately owned)

127 (below, right). Patchwork "show towel," Le Moyne Star, made by Euphemia Kichline, c. 1838, probably Pennsylvania. 32″ × 16″. This show towel has been included since it is an unusual example of the use of patchwork, which alternates here with heavily embroidered roses. (Privately owned)

128 (left). Patchwork quilt, Star of Bethlehem with diamond border, c. 1850. 115¼″ × 113″. Nearly all parts of the design are made of printed calicoes. The quilt was made by Sophonisba Peale, daughter of Charles Willson Peale. (Philadelphia Museum of Art)

129 (left). Patchwork quilt, Mosaic (also called Honeycomb and Flower Garden), c. 1850. 96″ × 84″. The design has been created entirely with hundreds and hundreds of 1¼″ hexagonal blocks of printed cottons, some glazed. Various forms of stars were made by using dark and light patches. (Henry Ford Museum)

130 (above). Patchwork quilt, Lone Star, c. 1850, made by a slave owned by Mrs. Jane Greer Jackson of Lebanon, Tennessee. 86″ × 81″. The pieced squares are small and closely quilted. The wide outside border is trapunto work. (San Antonio Museum Association)

131 (opposite). Detail of a patchwork quilt, Star of the East, c. 1840. 75″ × 75″. The entire quilt is composed of squares, with the plain ones quilted in a feather-wreath pattern. (Denver Art Museum)

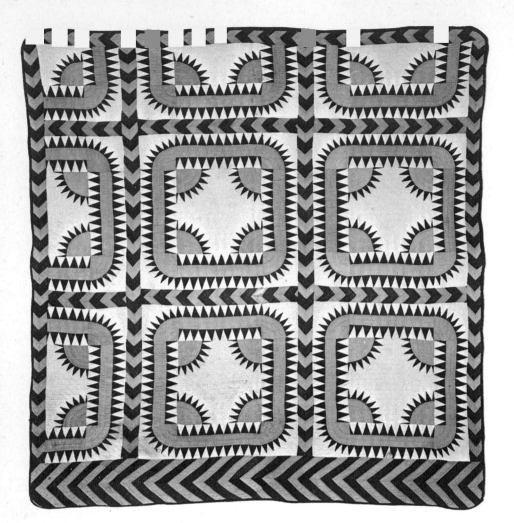

132 (above). Patchwork quilt, unnamed design, c. 1800.
75″ × 71¾″. An unusual design using many patches.
One of the finest examples of American patchwork art
to be found. (Rhea Goodman: Quilt Gallery, Inc.)

133 (right). Patchwork quilt with appliqué center and a series
of borders, c. 1835, Pennsylvania (?). 75½″ × 71¾″.
Printed and plain cottons have been used in an improvised
rural manner. (Rhea Goodman: Quilt Gallery, Inc.)

134 (opposite). Patchwork quilt, unnamed design, c. 1850,
New York (?). 102½″ × 74½″. In the catalogue for the
famous collection of quilts at Shelburne Museum in Vermont,
Lilian Baker Carlisle calls a quilt similar to this one
"New York Beauty," for it was found in Setauket,
Long Island. This splendid coverlet surely deserves an
equally glowing title. (Privately owned)

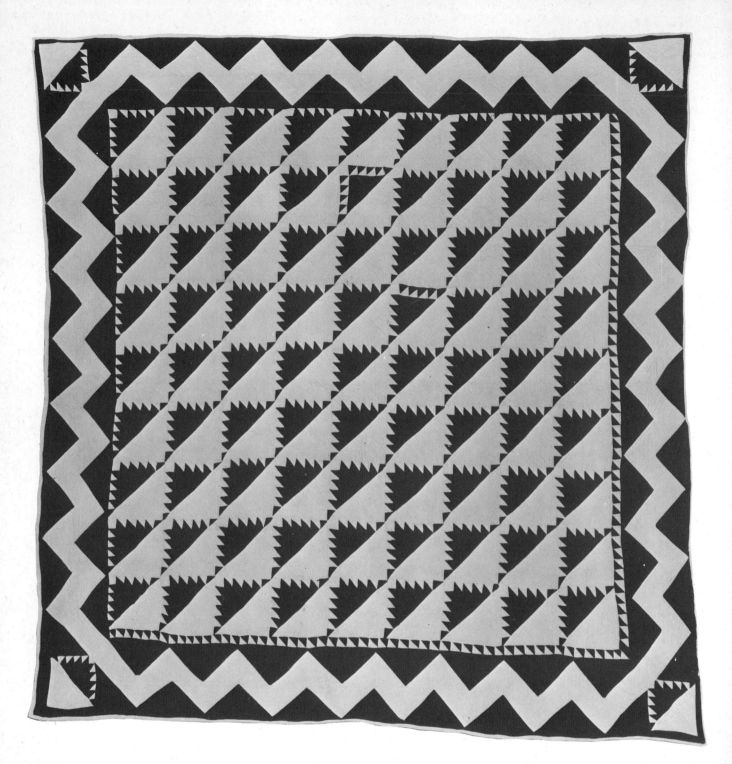

135 (above). Patchwork quilt, Sawtooth or Kansas Troubles, c. 1840. 76½" × 75½".
The making of this dark-blue-and-white quilt was a real exercise in patience.
Note the three places where errors were made in the direction of the "teeth."
(George Schoellkopf: The Peaceable Kingdom, Ltd.)

136 (left). Patchwork quilt, Complex T, c. 1850. 88½″ × 79½″. Perhaps a "one of a kind" design that forms the letter **T** on a diagonal and reversed. The colors are olive green and white. (Rhea Goodman: Quilt Gallery, Inc.)

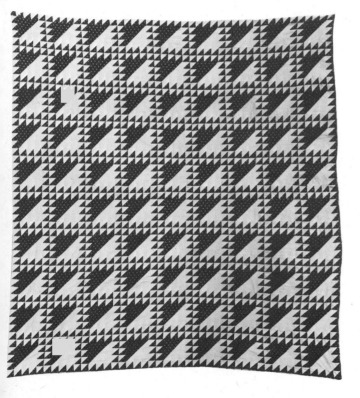

138 (above). Detail of a patchwork quilt, Arabic Lattice, c. 1850. 80″ × 70″. A pattern created in much the same way as figure 136 above, with a positive and a negative arranged with no waste. (Henry Ford Museum)

137 (above). Patchwork quilt, Sawtooth, c. 1840. 78″ × 65″. Compared with the quilt on page 106, this is a more professional handling of a complicated technical problem. The double rows of "teeth" make the design a very strong one. (Privately owned)

139 (above). Patchwork quilt, Wild Goose Chase, c. 1830. 95" × 80½". The feathered-circle quilting in the white squares is a pleasant use of curved lines to contrast with the diamond shapes of the patches. (Mr. and Mrs. Donald Morris)

141 (left). Patchwork quilt, Wild Goose Chase, c. 1830. 82″ × 82″. The muted reds, browns, and grays of the fabrics in this quilt give it a decidedly rural flavor. (George Schoellkopf: The Peaceable Kingdom, Ltd.)

143 (above). Patchwork quilt, unnamed design, c. 1860, Pennsylvania. 72″ × 72″. A very handsome quilt in the typical dark, intense colors used by the Amish sect in Pennsylvania. (George Schoellkopf: The Peaceable Kingdom, Ltd.)

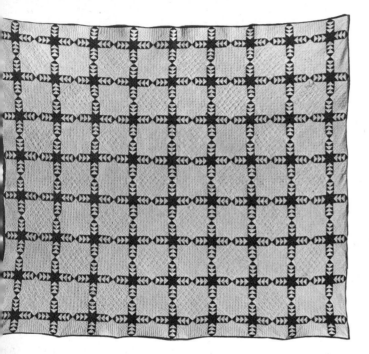

140 (opposite, below). Patchwork quilt, Storm at Sea (variation), c. 1840. 83″ × 68″. Squares and diamonds combine here to create a sense of curving lines. (Mr. and Mrs. Donald Morris)

142 (above). Patchwork quilt, Geese in Flight, c. 1847. 87½″ × 80″. Made on the Day Pattison Plantation in Alexandria, Louisiana. Much of the white area is pieced. There are reputedly 3,600 pieces in the quilt. (San Antonio Museum Association)

144 (above). Patchwork quilt, unnamed design, c. 1850. 84″ × 83″. Diagonal bands set in squares. Since most of the fabrics are striped the result is striking. (Privately owned)

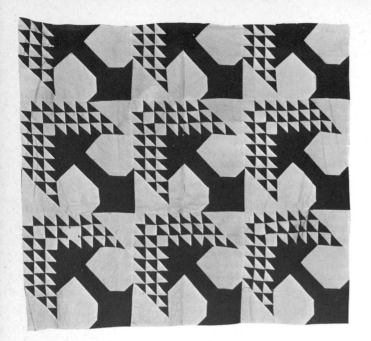

145 (left). Detail of a patchwork quilt, Tree of Life or Pine Tree, 1875–1900. 80″ × 68″. This is an early Massachusetts pattern that has often been copied. (Henry Ford Museum)

146 (below). Patchwork quilt, Tree of Life (variation), c: 1860. 85″ × 69½″. The squares containing the trees are set as diamonds in the quilt and alternate with plain squares, thus making the trees grow neatly in rows. (Mr. and Mrs. Donald Morris)

147 (opposite). Patchwork quilt, Tree of Life. This quilt was started in 1880 and completed in 1919 in Dearborn, Michigan. 88¾″ × 71″. The trees are composed of large patches and effectively face both sides of the spread. (Henry Ford Museum)

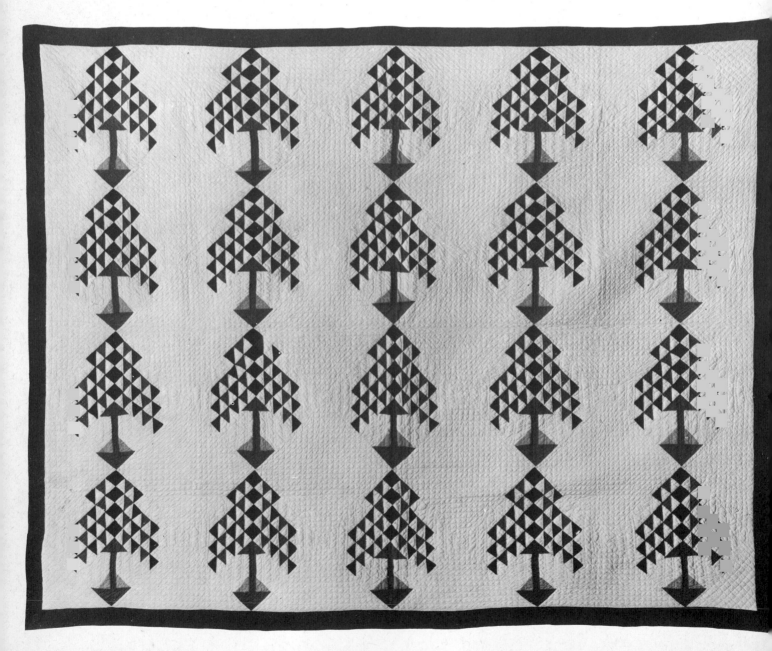

148 (above). Patchwork and appliqué marriage quilt, dated
1785, Maine. 86″ × 81″. The center square carries the
following inscription between the four hearts: "Anna Tuels
her bed quilt given to her by her mother in the year
Au 23 1785." The wide quilted border is of pink calandered
wool, and the patches are of both printed and
woven fabrics. (Wadsworth Atheneum)

149 (right), 149a (opposite, below). Patchwork quilt,
Double Nine Patch, c. 1825. 99″ × 82″. The fabric used for
the patches in this quilt seems to be an early, exotic print.
It makes a lacy contrast to the heavy trapunto work
in the white blocks using such designs as pineapple, wreath,
flower, and leaf. The quilt is initialed "R D."
(Denver Art Museum)

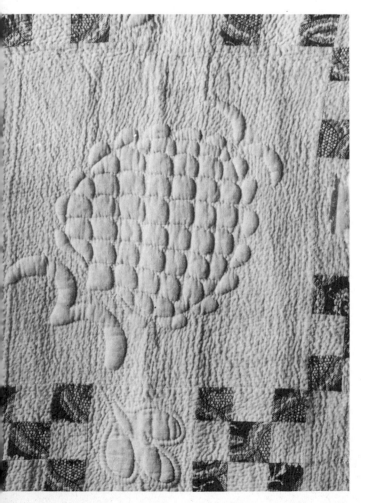

150 (above, center). Patchwork quilt, Feathered Square, c. 1845. 84" × 82". The simple patchwork in soft pink and white is a suitable frame for the finely drafted quilting of plumes and feather circles. (Rhea Goodman: Quilt Gallery, Inc.)

151 (above). Patchwork quilt, Pinwheel, c. 1785, Virginia. 100¾" × 100". This large quilt is made up of a series of simple borders of printed linens and toiles. The center is a fragment of a toile called "Penn's Treaty with the Indians." This quilt was made by Martha Washington and given to her niece, Mrs. Tobias Lear. (The Mount Vernon Ladies' Association of the Union)

152 (above, left). Patchwork quilt, unnamed design, c. 1830, Pennsylvania (?). 91″ × 90¾″. Formal symmetrical floral spray with stems and leaves appliquéd. Quilting in alternate blocks in a feather circle. The quilting in the wide border is in an undulating design. (Rhea Goodman: Quilt Gallery, Inc.)

153 (left). Detail of a patchwork quilt, Tulip (later called Virginia Lily or North Carolina Lily), c. 1820. 92″ × 89″. A Pennsylvania German style of patching and quilting. The colors are red, yellow, and green on white cotton. A wide border of quilting is set apart from the patchwork by a triangle or sawtooth border. (Philadelphia Museum of Art)

154 (center). Patchwork quilt, Tulip or Peony, c. 1820, Pennsylvania (?). 94″ × 75″. This design is based on the Le Moyne Star with appliqué stems and leaves. The calyx and stems are green, and the red flowers are of a slightly patterned calico. (Henry Ford Museum)

155 (above, right). Patchwork quilt, Virginia Lily or North Carolina Lily, c. 1820. 81″ × 78″. The pattern is a combination of patchwork and appliqué. The border is innovative, but it obviously proved to be a problem to make the four corners alike! (Denver Art Museum)

156 (below, right). Patchwork and appliqué quilt, Cactus Rose or Peony, c. 1840, Pennsylvania (?). 84″ × 83″. A bright, colorful piece using the eight-pointed star of figure 154 with two points removed to allow for the stem and leaves. (Rhea Goodman: Quilt Gallery, Inc.)

157 (above). Patchwork quilt, Flower Basket, c. 1830, New England. 83″ × 75″.
Many variations of this pattern are recorded, some with fruit and some with flowers.
These baskets are made of red and green blocks, and the framework is red and white.
(Henry Ford Museum)

158 (below). Patchwork quilt, Peony or Lily, with the quilted inscription, "Emeline Talbott Montgomery Co. Maryland Oct 10th, 1844." 94¼″ × 94″. An elaborate version of the Tulip pattern carried out in fine detail in patchwork and appliqué. The colors are blue and red against a yellowed-white background. (Privately owned)

159 (above). Patchwork and appliqué quilt, c. 1825. 80″ × 76″. The red and green of the patchwork and appliqué border give a light, cheery feeling to this piece. (Privately owned)

160 (below). Patchwork and appliqué quilt, Tulip, made by Saiddie Ford, age 67, of West Hope, Henry Co., Ohio, 1882. 88″ × 70″. A very bold, angular version of the tulip pattern with fine feather quilting. (Privately owned)

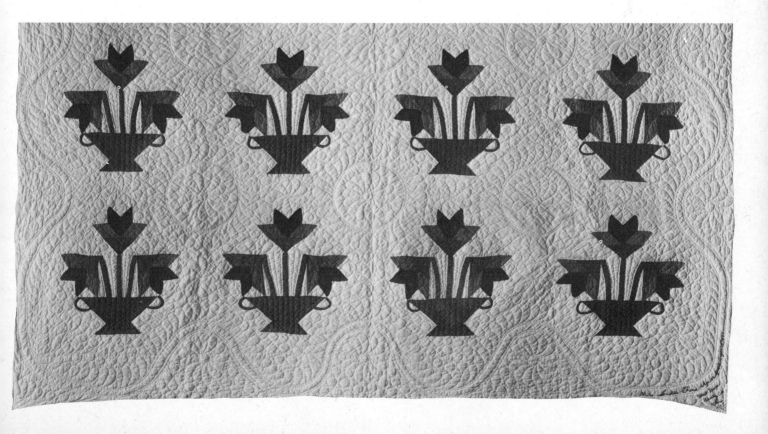

161 (above, left). Patchwork quilt, Criss-Cross, c. 1915, Amish. 76″ × 75″. Made by a Mrs. Stoltzfus of Elverson, Lancaster County, Pennsylvania, for her daughter, Rebecca. A splendid combination of unusual colors. (Sarah Melvin)

162 (left). Patchwork quilt, Double Irish Chain, c. 1915, Amish. 86½″ × 84¼″. Made by Mrs. Stoltzfus for her son, Brownie. Brilliant three-color harmony with feather-scroll quilting. (Sarah Melvin)

163 (above), 163a (opposite, above right). Patchwork quilt, unnamed design, c. 1860.
97¾" × 88". A symmetrically designed quilt using patches of various shapes and
in various combinations. The use of hearts and hexagons in the design scheme
suggests a Pennsylvania origin. Both plain and printed fabrics have been used.
This handsome coverlet is particularly interesting in that a Bible verse has been
inscribed in India ink on each of the white patches found in the center of the
large patchwork blocks. Quilts inscribed in this way are often known as "Scripture"
quilts. The verse written on the white patch in the detail illustrated on page 118
reads as follows: "The wilderness, and the solitary place, shall be glad for them and
the desert shall rejoice, and blossom as the rose." (George Schoellkopf: The Peaceable
Kingdom, Ltd.)

164 (right). Patchwork and appliqué quilt, Whig's Defeat, c. 1850. 79″ × 77″. This quilt is an exercise in politics and patriotism. The patchwork design in rose on a beige ground is named after the Whig Party that Henry Clay tried to consolidate as a Presidential candidate in 1844. The party finally disintegrated when it was sundered by sectional interests in the 1852 Presidential election. The printed materials appliquéd on the spread depict Washington, Clay, and General Zachary Taylor. The following poem is inscribed in ink underneath the flag, which is embroidered with thirty-one stars: "As long as thy waves shall gleam in the Sun,/ And long as thy Heroes remember their Scars,/ Be the hands of Thy Children united as one,/ And peace shed Her Light on the Banner of Stars.// Hail! Thou Republic of Washington, Hail!/ Never may Star of thy Union wax pale,/ Hope of the World! may each Omen of ill,/ Fade in the light of thy Destiny still." (Privately owned)

166 (below). Lining of a patchwork quilt, c. 1800. This lining was made by piecing together several "Declaration of Independence" kerchiefs with a "James Garfield for President" portrait. (Henry Ford Museum)

165 (above), 165a (opposite). Patchwork quilt, 1800–1810. 97½″ × 96″. A rare example of early patchwork quilting, notable for the eighteenth-century printed cottons used for the two wide borders and the patches. The centerpiece of this quilt is a printed souvenir handkerchief titled "The Death of General Washington." Surrounding the deathbed scene are the familiar exalted phrases eulogizing the great man, one of which calls him "the Favourite of the Genius of Liberty." (Privately owned)

167 (right), 167a (below). Patchwork quilt, unnamed design, c. 1860. 87½″ × 77″. An eight-sided figure enclosed in a square, and composed of octagons, diamonds, and squares in two colors and white. (Henry Ford Museum)

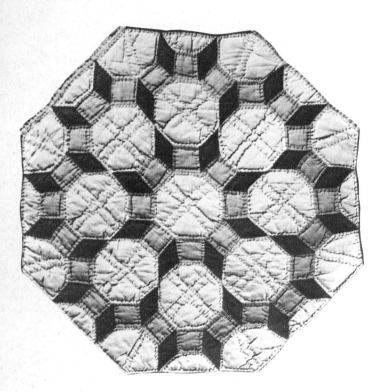

168 (right). Patchwork quilt, Steeple Chase, c. 1865. 81″ × 69″. An easy, effective pattern with no attempt at originality. This example is made up of more than twenty different dark-blue and white figured calicoes. (Denver Art Museum)

169 (opposite). Patchwork and appliqué quilt, Sunburst, c. 1840. 87½″ × 70″. A variety of small-figured red calicoes are used in the medallions. The triple-stripe border provides effective contrast to the "wheel" around each sunburst. (Rhea Goodman: Quilt Gallery, Inc.)

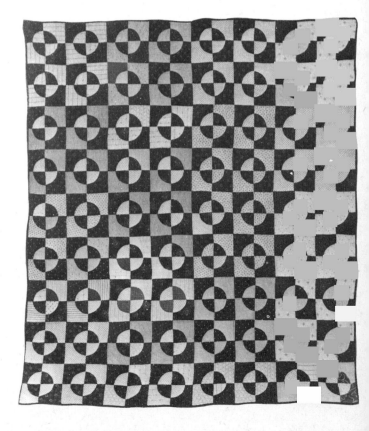

170 (above). Patchwork quilt, Log Cabin, c. 1890. 68″ × 60″. Lights and darks have been arranged to form a giant horizontal zigzag using wools and silks. This piece is not quilted but is properly described as "tufted." (Henry Ford Museum)

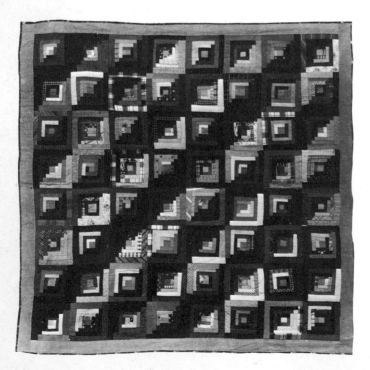

171 (left). Patchwork quilt, Log Cabin, c. 1920. 72″ × 72″: Lights and darks are here arranged to make diagonals across the whole spread. Silk has been "tied" or tufted to a silk backing. (Henry Ford Museum)

172 (center). Patchwork quilt, Log Cabin, c. 1890. 53½″ × 51½″. Lights and darks arranged to form concentric diamonds, thus giving the name "Barn Raising" to this variation on the Log Cabin type. (Rhea Goodman: Quilt Gallery, Inc.)

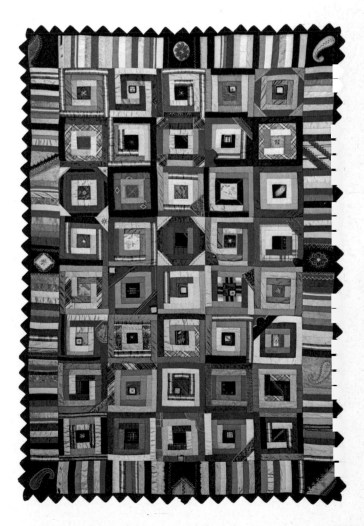

173 (above, right). Patchwork quilt, Log Cabin, c. 1850.
56½″ × 56½″. Lights and darks arranged in this way are
known as "Windmill Blades." (Rhea Goodman:
Quilt Gallery, Inc.)

174 (right). Patchwork quilt, Log Cabin (variation), c. 1900.
63″ × 43″. The use of "Crazy quilt" effects and
embroidery add to the unique quality of this example.
(Rhea Goodman: Quilt Gallery, Inc.)

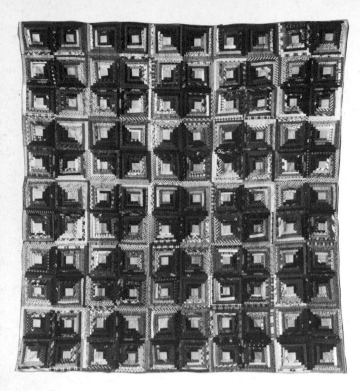

175 (left). Patchwork quilt, Log Cabin, c. 1890. 76″ × 76″.
Darks and lights are arranged here to form a checkerboard.
Each block was started with a "turkey red" wool square.
Wools and silks used. (Henry Ford Museum)

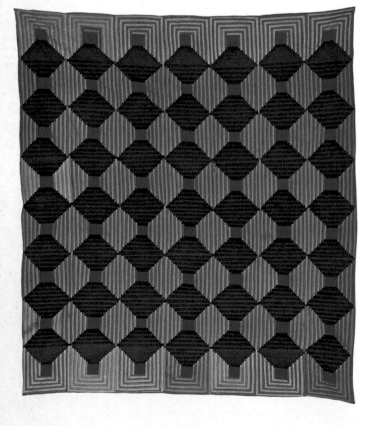

176 (left). Patchwork quilt, Log Cabin (variation), c. 1870.
87″ × 76″. A colorful and different interpretation
of the Log Cabin style, where the dark elements of
the design appear to be suspended on a wide red ribbon.
(Betty Sterling: Brainstorm Farm)

177 (above). Patchwork quilt, Log Cabin, c. 1890,
Gardiner, Maine. 68″ × 66″. The basic unit of this silk
quilt is a hexagon rather than a square. The result
is an elegantly rich and complex design. (Philadelphia
Museum of Art)

178 (above). Patchwork quilt, Log Cabin, c. 1890. 78½″ × 67″. Light and dark, plain and printed fabrics form a checkerboard here, called "Courthouse Steps." All of the foregoing examples of the Log Cabin style are best called "throws," since they are not quilted, but, instead, are joined together with tufting. (Rhea Goodman: Quilt Gallery, Inc.)

179 (above). Patchwork quilt, c. 1870. 89″ × 82″. Composed entirely of squares set together to create an expanding diamond design of exciting color combinations. Unusual in that this quilt is one of a pair. (Privately owned)

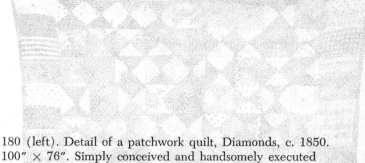

180 (left). Detail of a patchwork quilt, Diamonds, c. 1850. 100″ × 76″. Simply conceived and handsomely executed with a nice selection of printed patches. (Henry Ford Museum)

181 (left). Patchwork quilt top, Triangles, c. 1840. 74″ × 70″. An unquilted top depending entirely on the right choice of patches to accent one another in a handsome design. (Rhea Goodman: Quilt Gallery, Inc.)

182 (above). Detail of a patchwork quilt, unnamed design, c. 1840. 88″ × 70″. A pattern made of hexagons composed of triangles with one point changed in color. Stripes enliven the effect of the pattern. (Henry Ford Museum)

183 (left). Patchwork cradle quilt, Bow Tie
(variation), c. 1830. 41″ × 31″. The great variety of
prints used in this quilt suggests a rural origin,
where even patches were reused. (Privately owned)

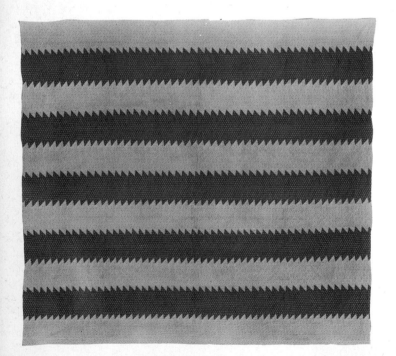

184 (left). Patchwork quilt, Tree Everlasting, c. 1885.
85½″ × 77½″. Two small calico patterns in red and
yellow are used to make this effective, simple
design. (Rhea Goodman: Quilt Gallery, Inc.)

185 (above). Patchwork quilt, Goose in the Pond or
Young Man's Fancy, c. 1900. 75″ × 62″. A country
quilt in many printed calicoes and checks.
(Henry Ford Museum)

186 (below). Patchwork quilt, unnamed design, c. 1840. 83″ × 63″. An effective and charming design utilizing large and small squares in a diamond pattern. (Mr. and Mrs. Michael D. Hall)

187 (right). Detail of a patchwork quilt, Double Wedding Ring, c. 1920. 84″ × 70″. An effective and popular design when carefully drafted and patched. Examples of this design are usually poorly executed. (Henry Ford Museum)

188 (below). Patchwork quilt, Nine Patch, c. 1825. 96″ × 94″. The nine-patch blocks have been set diagonally and are separated by green calico bands. (Henry Ford Museum)

189 (left). Patchwork quilt, Nine Patch, c. 1830. 85″ × 78″. Nine-patch blocks alternate here with one-color blocks. The fabrics are mostly blue-and-brown dress prints. (Henry Ford Museum)

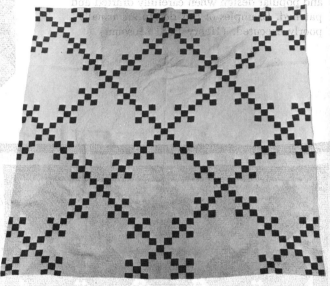

190 (below). Patchwork quilt top, unnamed design, c. 1870. 87½″ × 86″. (Sarah Melvin)

191 (above). Patchwork quilt, Puss in the Corner (also Double Nine Patch or Burgoyne's Surrender), c. 1825. 99″ × 99″. (Old Economy Village)

192 (opposite, above right). Patchwork quilt, Baby Blocks, c. 1870. 54″ × 52″. A collection of bright-colored silks in solid colors and prints compose this fascinating mosaic. (Henry Ford Museum)

193 (opposite, below), 193a (opposite, above left). Patchwork quilt, Stair Steps or Illusion (among many other names), c. 1890. 87″ × 66″. Stripes add to the optical tricks this design plays. A fine example of a very exacting pattern requiring careful planning and "sewmanship." (Rhea Goodman: Quilt Gallery, Inc.)

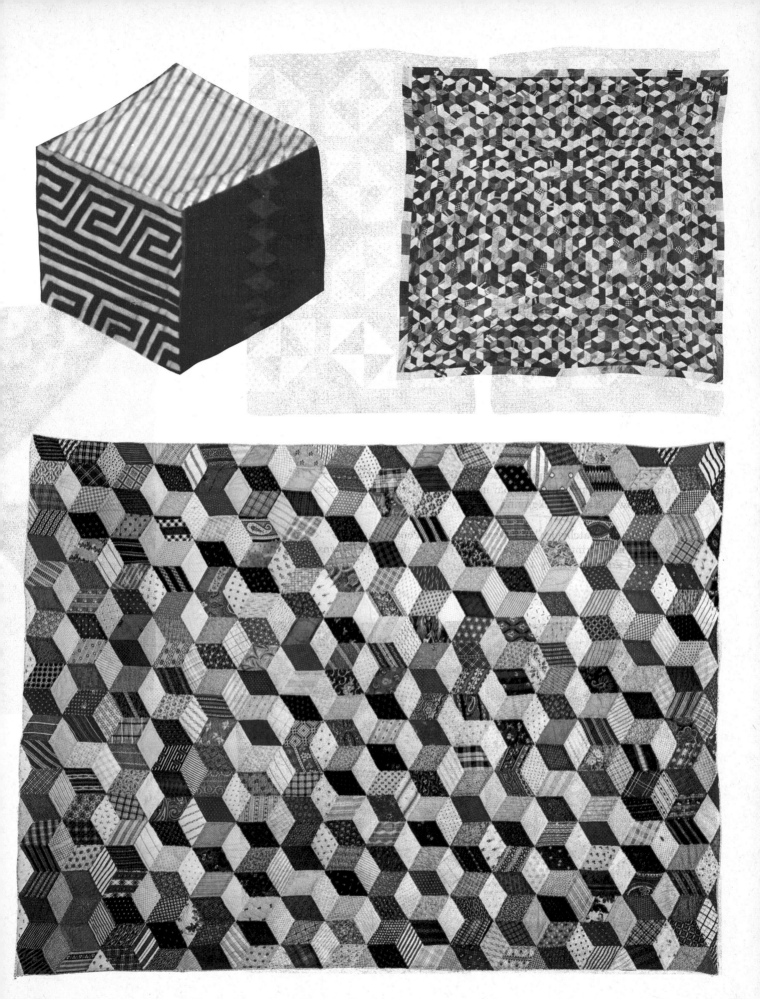

133

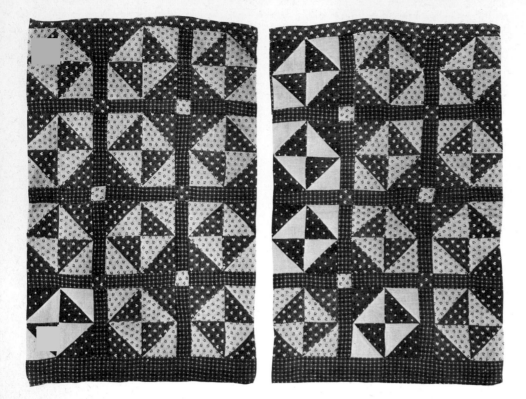

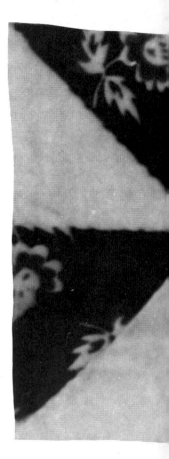

194 (above). Patchwork pillowcases, c. 1850, Pennsylvania. 26¼″ × 17¼″.
Patched in a variation of Cross-Bar in red, yellow, and green calicoes
on a brown-striped background. (Henry Ford Museum)

195 (below). "Patchwork" pillowcases, c. 1825, Pennsylvania. 23″ × 15½″.
Glazed chintz printed in a simulated patchwork design in browns,
reds, and greens. (Henry Ford Museum)

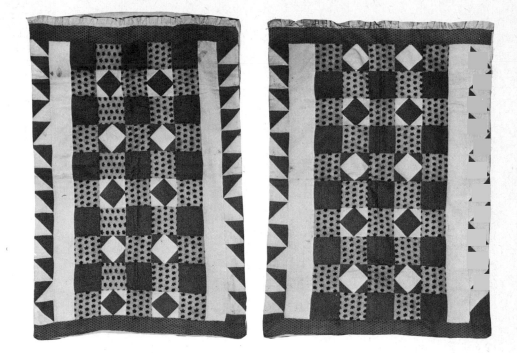

196 (above). Patchwork pillowcases, c. 1850, Pennsylvania. 32½″ × 22″. Coarsely patched printed calicoes and plain pink cotton make up an unnamed design. There is a small ruffled trim at the open end. (Henry Ford Museum)

197 (below), 197a (center). Patchwork pillowcases, c. 1830, Pennsylvania. 24¼″ × 17″. The design is a simple pinwheel in red and brown floral prints against white. (Henry Ford Museum)

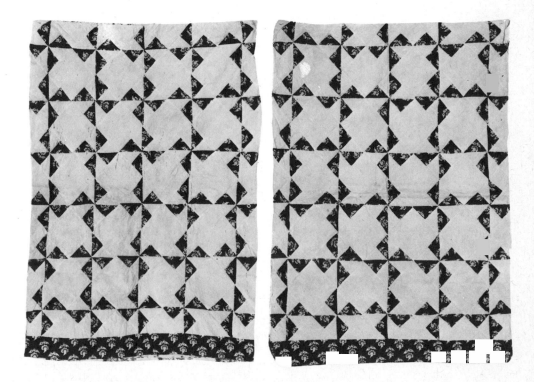

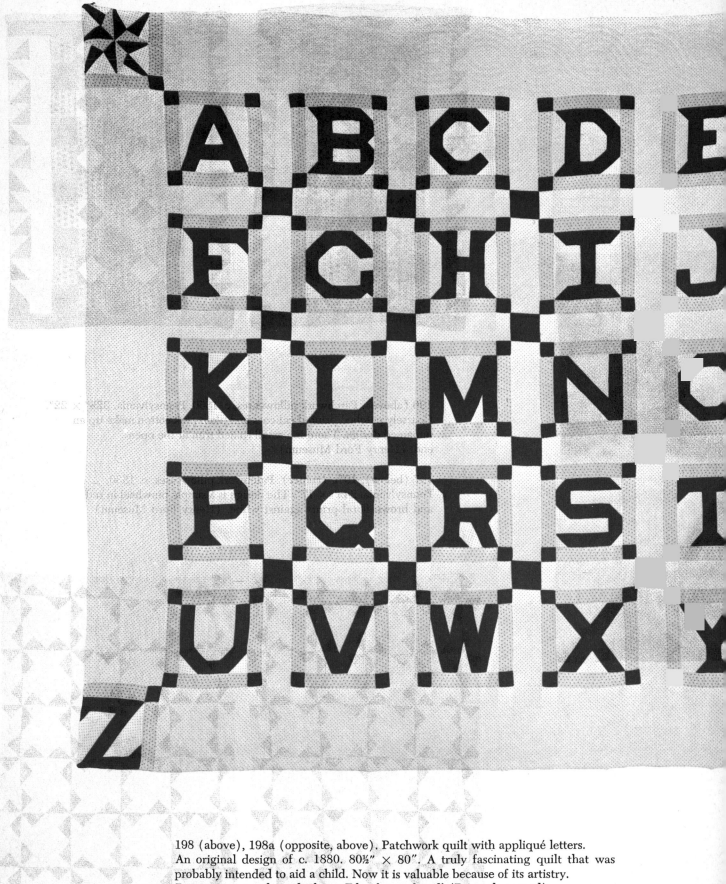

198 (above), 198a (opposite, above). Patchwork quilt with appliqué letters.
An original design of c. 1880. 80½″ × 80″. A truly fascinating quilt that was
probably intended to aid a child. Now it is valuable because of its artistry.
Be sure to note where the letter Z has been placed! (Privately owned)

199 (below). Patchwork quilt of original design, dated August 9, 1848, made by
Jane D. Waldron, Castile, New York. 84″ × 75″. Jane Waldron was born in 1828
in England. She taught school in Castile, New York, and was married in Michigan
at the age of twenty-four. The letter patches are made of red calico, ¾″ square or
¾″ × 1½″. From the Peck collection. This is one of the rarest quilts known.
(Julia Boyer Reinstein)

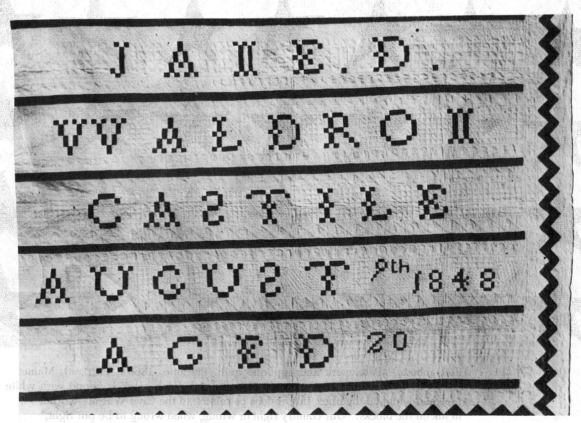

200 (above). Patchwork and appliqué quilt, Patriotic, 1860's, Portland, Maine. 81" × 71". The stars are alternately blue and red. Each block is bound with white tape and whipped together. Inscriptions pertaining to the Civil War are written in ink on the blocks: "Our country right or wrong, when wrong to be put right, when right to be kept right," "Abraham Lincoln knows the ropes! All our hopes center about the brave and true. Let us help him all we can," "While our fingers guide the needle, our thoughts are intense (in tents!)." (Privately owned)

201 (below). Patchwork and appliqué quilt, Patriotic, c. 1900. Dimensions unavailable. A simple, balanced design in red, white, and blue that is elegant in its clarity and forthrightness. Photograph courtesy Gary C. Cole. (Privately owned)

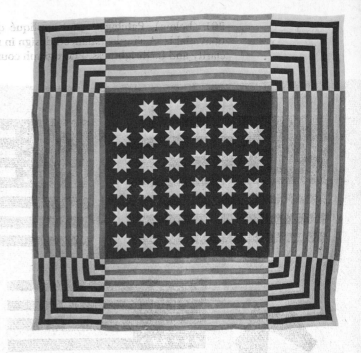

202 (above), 202a (left). Patchwork quilt, Patriotic, c. 1890 (?), Hawaii. 92″ × 89¾″. Strips of plain red, white, and blue fabric are stitched together not as in a flag, but simply to form a strong design. The stars are eight-pointed, but the fact that there are thirty-four of them appears to have no special significance. (Privately owned)

204 (below), 204a (right). Patchwork quilt, Patriotic,
c. 1900, Hawaii. 90″ × 88″. A simply arranged design
based on the Hawaiian and American flags. Since each of
the American flags contains thirteen stars, it is obviously
meant to symbolize the original Thirteen Colonies. (Privately
owned)

203 (opposite, below). Detail of a patchwork quilt,
Patriotic, c. 1930. 96″ × 90″. A naïvely embroidered
Statue of Liberty is surrounded by appliquéd and patched
five-pointed stars in red, white, and blue. The overall
quilting is coarse. (Henry Ford Museum)

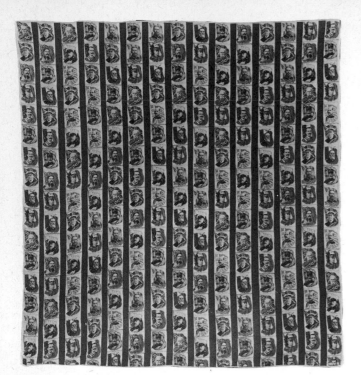

205 (left), 205a (opposite). Patchwork quilt, c. 1920. 73" × 67". This polychrome quilt consists of labels from tobacco pouches that have been sewn together in vertical strips and the strips joined with dividers of plain red cotton. Feather stitching has been added to cover the joining of the labels, which depict several public worthies at the time of World War I, including General Joffre of France, Victor Emmanuel II of Italy, Lord Kitchener of England, Gustav of Sweden, Alphonso XIII of Spain, etc. (Rhea Goodman: Quilt Gallery, Inc.)

206 (left). Patchwork bedcover, c. 1920. 68" × 52". The patches are made of felt printed with the flags of many countries and with blanket designs of some American Indian tribes. These patches were printed in many sizes and colors and given out with cigars. (Henry Ford Museum)

207 (above). Patchwork quilt, Patriotic c. 1890, Hawaii. 78"½ × 77½". The royal crown of Hawaii is worked into an effective red, white, and blue design repeating the Hawaiian flag. The quilting is done in diagonal parallel lines. This spread belonged to a royalist family in Hawaii. (Betty Sterling: Brainstorm Farm)

208 (above), 208a, 208b, 208c (opposite). Appliqué coverlet, known as the "Westover–Berkeley" coverlet, c. 1770, Virginia. 105½″ × 97¾″. The background of this large spread is of natural cotton pieced together with narrow bands of a red-and-white calico print. The border is made of a double band of fabric with the corners cut out to fit a four-posted bed. The appliqué is chintz, and there are many additions of elaborate embroidery, examples of which can be seen in the three details shown on page 145. The story of the making of this coverlet is told in the text for this chapter. (Valentine Museum)

THE APPLIQUÉ QUILT

Appliqué is the second great category of quiltmaking, and it was equally popular with patchwork in America during the same hundred-year span of 1775–1875. As we have already seen, the technique of patchwork involves assembling hundreds of individual patches side by side into a large, overall design. In the appliqué technique the various elements of the design, such as hearts, flowers, leaves, birds, vases, are cut from various fabrics and sewn onto the background fabric of the spread with a simple seed, buttonhole, or overcasting stitch. (The edges of the design elements are turned under, in the form of a hem, before stitching.)

Early writers about quilts stated that the appliqué type followed patchwork because quiltmakers became bored with having to sew in straight lines. There is a point here, but the quality of workmanship in an appliqué quilt is usually so far superior to that found in patchwork, that one could make a case for its having preceded it. Certainly the most elaborate and intricate quilts available for study are in the appliqué category, and there was a tendency in the nineteenth century for the quality of workmanship to decline.

The earliest appliqué coverlets were created by sewing design elements cut from printed chintzes and imported Oriental calicoes to white cotton or linen spreads, and then elaborately quilting them so as to enhance the motifs in the printed fabrics. These spreads were sometimes further decorated with fine embroidery in cotton or silk to supply the detail lost in trimming the patches before sewing them to the white spread. A perfect example of this style is the "Wedding Quilt" in the collection of the Hennepin County Historical Society in Minneapolis, Minnesota. This quilt has been a frequent prizewinner in competitions principally because of its excellent design. The flowers have been cut from an early chintz and individually grouped and sewn onto the white background to form the wreath, the center medallions, and the garlands in the border. After each detail of the design was stitched in place, the background was quilted with a delicate cross-hatching. In old records from along the

209 (above). Appliqué quilt, using calico and chintz in reds and tans, probably 1920's. 78½" × 75½". Presumably made to delight a child, the spiral design of this charming spread ably evokes the illusion of the animals marching two-by-two into Noah's Ark. (Privately owned)

210 (above). Appliqué quilt of doves with flower offerings, c. 1850. 81" × 75". Possibly made in Pennsylvania, the appliqué is in red and two shades of green. The delightful crudity of the piece gives it a true folk-art quality. (Privately owned)

eastern seaboard, where the Indian palampores and English chintzes were imported, such coverlets are often termed "Broderie Perse," indicating that fancy embroidery stitches were often added. Appliqué quilts in Pennsylvania often include embroidery in coarse wool.

The Valentine Museum in Richmond, Virginia, owns an outstanding spread of the type discussed above. It is the Westover—Berkeley coverlet. Made of fine unbleached cotton, it contains squares, triangles, and strips joined by narrow bands in a red calico print. The chintz appliqué and silk embroidery are very elaborate and were created by neighbors living in two of the great plantations on the James River in Virginia, from which the coverlet takes its name.

A document written September 8, 1946, by Susie McGuire Ellett describes this spread so well it deserves to be included here:

My son asked me to write down the history of the "Westover—Berkeley" spread which came to me on Mother's death. Her sister-in-law, my father's sister, Aunt Lucy McGuire, gave it to her before she died, and Mother always treasured it as one of her most valued heirlooms.

It was made somewhere before the time of the Revolution (because the beautiful Evelyn Byrd is supposed to have stitched one of the squares) by the ladies of Westover and Berkeley, the Byrds and the Harrisons. Their custom was to meet every fortnight under the Trysting Tree weather permitting, and sew on the spread. The Trysting Tree was situated somewhere on the boundary line between the two places, but in case of wet weather they met at one or the other of the "great houses."

The designs were cut from English chintz and appliquéd in colored silks onto fine unbleached cotton, and each four corners which formed a square within a square were sewed together with strips of red and white calico. The colors are remarkably clear still and the sprays of pink roses caught with tiny blue bows . . . the pineapples in four of the corners, the emblem of hospitality, and the cornucopias, or horns of plenty in four other corners are beautifully done. There are sprays of hops and tiny birds on trailing branches of flowers and a chipmunk, done entirely in embroidery. Around the whole there used to be a valance of hand-crocheted lace, but when that became tattered Aunt Lucy cut it off before she gave it to Mother.

My grandmother, Mary Willing Harrison, who was the daughter of the last Benjamin Harrison to own Berkeley (the 7th, I think) and the great-granddaughter of Mary Willing, the second wife of Col. William Byrd III of Westover, from whom the spread descended, used it always on her own bed, and Aunt Lucy had it on the bed when Father brought Mother, as a bride, to visit her and Uncle Edward. To carry on the tradition, Mother had it on our bed when Taze and I returned from our wedding trip!

Ever since, it has been kept wrapt in a towel and put carefully away in a chest. It is remarkably well pre-

211 (below). Appliqué quilt, c. 1850, Hawaii. 83¾" × 80". Completely typical of the Hawaiian style of quiltmaking, this handsome example consists of five, large, intricately cut blocks of pale apricot material sewn to a plain white background. The lines of quilting closely follow the irregular contours of the design elements. Nearly all Hawaiian quilts were given special names by their creators, and it was considered very bad manners to appropriate without permission a design created by someone else. The inspiration for this quilt appears to have been natural leaf and fruit forms. (Privately owned)

served, though there are some age spots, and some of the rose leaves, the embroidered veins, and the appliquing only remaining. Mary Willing Harrison was born at Westover, the great-granddaughter and namesake of old Mrs. Byrd who was still living at that time. Her mother, who was a daughter of Judge William Nelson of Yorktown, went to Grandmother's to have her first baby as her own mother was dead.

Every summer when Mother and I visited Aunt Lucy and Uncle Edward the spread would be brought out, and Aunt Lucy would tell us its history, but my children want it written down for them.

Mother remembers seeing the Trysting Tree, just a stump then, but still pointed out, when Father took her to Westover after they were married.

In addition to wedding quilts, there were friendship quilts (the joint work of the parish ladies of a church to be presented to their minister when he left for service elsewhere), freedom quilts (given to a young man upon reaching his twenty-first birthday), and family-record quilts with every block picturing a family event. Album quilts might contain beautiful renderings of the quilter's favorite flowers or the birds that visited her garden. Many of these album quilts are extraordinary for the delicacy of their inception and creation.

Many appliqué quilts are just as extraordinary for being superb examples of American folk art. In the Shelburne Museum there is an "Abraham Lincoln" spread that illustrates the Lincoln–Douglas debates. One of the greatest examples of quilted folk art is the spread from Greenfield Hill, Connecticut, that illustrates in appliqué a whole section of the town, showing the church with its minister and congregation, an inn with its sign, a school with dogs and children, and all manner of trees and flowers and birds. This coverlet was created from the greatest variety of scraps—homespun checks, India chintzes, stripes, and plain and printed cottons of every style.

One of the most interesting types of appliqué quilts developed in Hawaii in the early nineteenth century. When missionaries first came to the islands in 1820, tapa was the only form of fabric known. It was not a fabric cut to size, but was made from tree bark pounded and "felted" until it was of the size needed for a garment or a bedcover. Tapa was not washable, however, so the introduction of American fabrics was a most welcome innovation. The ladies of the Royal Household were the

212 (center), 212a (opposite). Album quilt combining appliqué work, embroidery, and trapunto quilting, which fills the spaces created by the serpentine garland in the wide border. 92″ × 91½″. This is a magnificent example of a Baltimore album quilt. The design, use of brilliant color, and execution of this spread are all quite breathtaking. It features public buildings and monuments (resplendent with eagles!) in Baltimore, one of which is shown in an enlarged detail on page 149. Refer back to the frontispiece on page 2 and the illustration on page 4 for details in color of some still lifes of fruit and flowers from this spread. (Privately owned)

first to learn quilting, but in a short time stitchery was taught to the children in the missionary schools. The first quilts were made of simple blocks of patchwork. But the beautiful countryside soon furnished ideas for designs in the appliqué style, and colors and contrasts became brilliant. Usually just two colors were used (or white and another color), and the design was cut in one large piece that filled the entire spread, as in typical Japanese cut-paper work. Designs also became very intricate and original in concept.

The Hawaiian quilts that are being made and sold to-day by professionals use a single large appliqué. The quilting style has changed since the first examples. It is now "contour" quilting with the lines of stitching about half an inch apart following the lines of the design until all the space is filled.

213 (above). Appliqué quilt, signed and dated 1807 by Esther S. Bradford of
Montville, Connecticut. 102″ × 99″. The extreme fineness of much of the appliqué work
makes it look as if the spread had been embroidered, but a magnifying glass will
soon prove it is really all appliqué! The inscription on the ribbon held by the
handsomely designed eagle reads: "Truth Is the Summum Bonum." On the ribbons
sprouting below the eagle we find: "Let the Arms of America Be Subjugated
Only to the Banners of the Cross and the Sweet Servitude of Immanuel.
His Yoke Is Easy and His Burden Light." (Henry Ford Museum)

214 (above), 214a (right). Appliqué summer bedcover, unquilted, c. 1810. 93½″ × 81″. The appliqué is of just one fabric, a block print in rose and blue-green on brown. The background of the coverlet is ecru cotton. The detail shows the printed pattern of the fabric. (The Stamford Historical Society, Inc.)

215 (above). Appliqué quilt, The Eagle's Nest, c. 1850,
Pennsylvania. 112″ × 104″. A highly original design with tiny
padded cherries depending from the tree branches, and five
padded blue eggs in the center. (San Antonio Museum Association)

216 (left). Appliqué cradle quilt, made as a gift.
22″ × 22″. Many of the blocks have been signed by
those who made them. (Henry Ford Museum)

217 (above), 217a (opposite, below right). Appliqué quilt, c. 1850, Pennsylvania German. 88½″ × 78″. Made in squares, each of which contains a sunflower in red and yellow. The hearts in the four corners of each block are red calico. Note the highly stylized birds in the serpentine border. (Titus C. Geesey Collection, Philadelphia Museum of Art)

153

218 (above). Appliqué quilt, c. 1810. 108″ × 108″. Two early printed cottons have been used for the appliqué designs. The eagle in the center is crowned with twenty-four stars. The series of borders are well planned and carried out, and the entire spread is enriched with trapunto work in a variety of designs. Photograph courtesy Ginsburg & Levy, Inc. (Privately owned)

219 (below). Appliqué quilt, with a patchwork border, c. 1850. 76″ × 69″. These four eagles with outstretched wings and shields on their bodies became very popular as a quilt pattern from Vermont to Ohio, as we can readily see from the other examples on page 155. This spread has been well executed in dark red, yellow, and beige against white. (George Schoellkopf: The Peaceable Kingdom, Ltd.)

220 (center). Appliqué and patchwork quilt, c. 1830, New England. 102″ × 97″. An early, handsomely styled spread using the eagle motif. The eagle has been cut from a light-brown calico and has a red-and-white shield emblazoned on its breast. The twenty-six dark-blue stars that surround him may or may not have some significance. The dark patchwork triangles are red, the light ones are pink, and the angled inner border is light blue. All the fabrics are printed. (Mrs. Jacob M. Kaplan)

221 (above). Appliqué quilt, c. 1850, Pennsylvania (?). 78″ × 78″. Four eagles, again with shields on their bodies, but now looking suspiciously like wild turkeys. An amusing version of the American eagle. (Henry Ford Museum)

222 (below). Appliqué summer coverlet, c. 1830, Pennsylvania. 86″ × 86″. Four eagles in bright-colored printed cottons have been joined here by eight more equally colorful eagles! Typically Pennsylvania in its design and execution. (Henry Ford Museum)

224 (right). Appliqué quilt, c. 1790, probably New York. 71½″ × 70″. A fascinating and impressive early example of appliqué combined with embroidery. It was probably inspired by a pattern book of the time. There are similar examples in museum collections. (Mr. and Mrs. Donald Morris)

223 (left), 223a (opposite). Appliqué quilt, Sunburst (variation), c. 1850. 77″ × 68″. The multicolored fabrics used in the design for this spread have been folded and sewn together to make "petals" that are raised above the surface of the spread. (Mr. and Mrs. James B. Boone, Jr.)

225 (right). Appliqué quilt, c. 1850, Pennsylvania German. 88″ × 87″. Done entirely in red and blue, this is an unusual arrangement of hearts, oak leaves, and berries. The berries are stuffed. The quilting of large and small leaf forms is well planned and executed. (Titus C. Geesey Collection, Philadelphia Museum of Art)

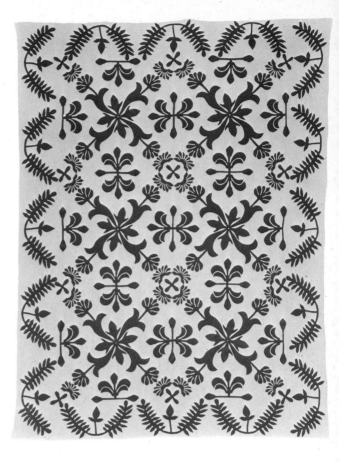

226 (above left). Appliqué quilt, Laurel Leaves, c. 1865. 93″ × 75½″. Napoleon's influence on American decorative art is reflected in this pattern, which is handsomely executed in red and green calicoes against white. Photograph courtesy George Schoellkopf: The Peaceable Kingdom, Ltd. (Privately owned)

227 (left). Appliqué and patchwork quilt, Rising Sun and Princess Feather combined, c. 1850, made by Mrs. Joshua Fitzgerald of Newark, New Jersey. 102″ × 93″ An elaborate and expertly executed quilt that won three state prizes in New Jersey. (The Newark Museum)

228 (above). Appliqué quilt, c. 1850. 100″ × 74″. The appliqué designs are done entirely in dark blue and set in a handsome overall pattern of almost classic regularity. (Cora Ginsburg)

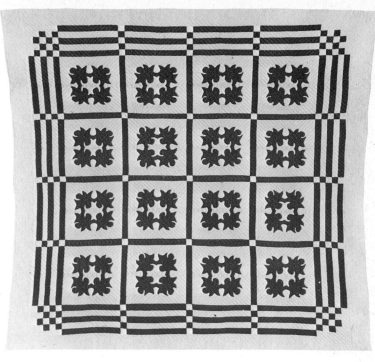

229 (right), 229a (below). Appliqué quilt with patchwork frames and border, c. 1937, called "a Kansas pattern" by its maker, Mrs. Charlotte Jane Whitehill. 91″ × 91″. The squares are quilted in a diagonal pattern, and the white border is quilted in a large floral design. (Denver Art Museum)

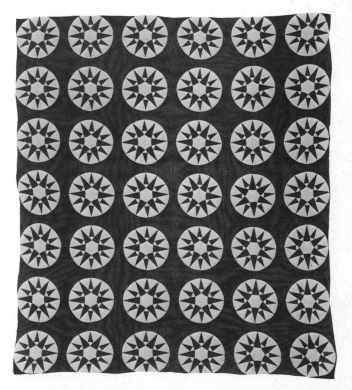

230 (right). Appliqué quilt with patchwork details, c. 1840, New England. 78″ × 66″. A variation of the Mariner's Compass pattern in dark blue and white, starting with a hexagonal center and ending in a circle. The quilting is in the form of concentric circles. (Rhea Goodman: Quilt Gallery, Inc.)

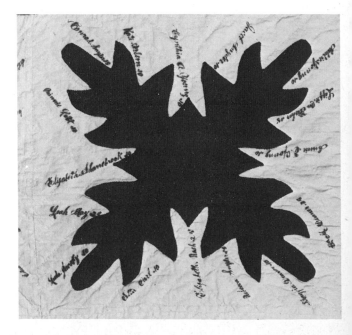

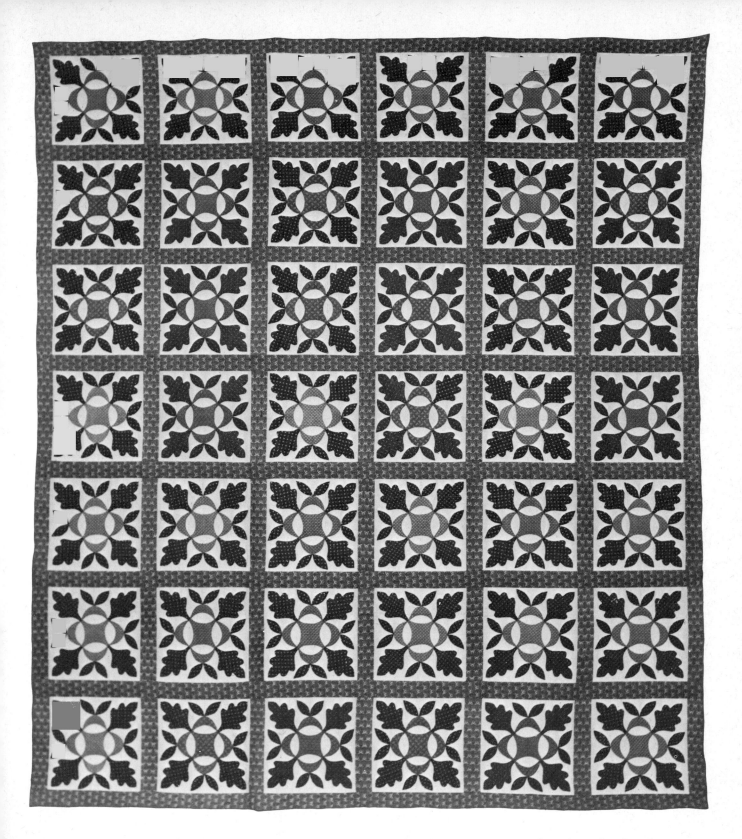

231 (opposite, above), 231a, 231b (opposite, below).
Appliqué quilt, Oak Leaf, c. 1860, probably Pennsylvania.
76″ × 74″. This red-and-white presentation quilt is
perhaps best described as a "tithing" quilt. Presented to the
Reverend E. J. Metzler (see figure 231a), possibly on
his retirement from the ministry. Each member of the
congregation has inscribed his or her name around the
appliqué designs (see figure 231b), together with the sum
of money pledged to the pastor—10¢, 15¢, 25¢!
(Betty Sterling: Brainstorm Farm)

232 (above). Appliqué quilt, Oak Leaf and Reel, c. 1840,
New England (?). 122″ × 104″. Three printed calicoes in
greens and reds are used to construct this large spread. It
seems certain that the appliqué designs were cut from new
cloth, for scraps that had been saved could not have produced
such a precise, neat result. The lining is stamped "New
Bedford Steam Mills." (Denver Art Museum)

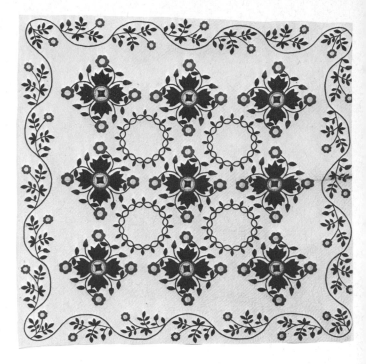

234 (above), 234a (left). Appliqué quilt, a Midwest version of Rose of Sharon, made by Mrs. Charlotte Jane Whitehill in 1932. 87″ × 87″. Handsomely drafted, this spread has been appliquéd with minute attention to color effects and closely quilted, using 1,419 yards of thread. (Denver Art Museum)

233 (above). Appliqué quilt, Oak Leaf (variation), c. 1850, New England (?). 85″ × 81″. An ambitious piece of work, but design sensitivity is lacking, and the handling of the meandering border is poor at the corners. (Henry Ford Museum)

235 (right). Appliqué quilt, Whig Rose, c. 1861. 82½″ × 73½″. The design has been worked into exacting squares with a lovely color harmony of bittersweet and yellow flowers with grayish yellow-green stems and leaves, all against white. Photograph courtesy Rhea Goodman: Quilt Gallery, Inc. (Privately owned)

236 (above). Appliqué quilt, Whig Rose (variation), c. 1861. 75″ × 75″.
By alternating the "Rose"-filled squares with the rose wreath, a lightness of effect
is achieved. (Mr. and Mrs. Donald Morris)

237 (left), 237a (opposite). Appliqué quilt, Autumn Leaf, made in 1934 by Mrs. Charlotte Jane Whitehill. 89" × 89". An exact copy of a quilt exhibited at the Chicago World's Fair in 1893. The "sewmanship" in this specimen speaks for itself in the illustration and in the enlarged detail on page 165. (Denver Art Museum)

239 (below). Detail of an appliqué quilt, Orange Slices or Reel, initialed and dated "E W 1818." 96" × 92". The wide border of an early printed chintz is an interesting feature, and the quilting is very fine. (Henry Ford Museum)

238 (above). Appliqué quilt, Basket, c. 1830. 99" × 99". Diagonal squares containing baskets filled with open blossoms and buds, alternating with squares of elaborately quilted floral designs. The grapes in the border are stuffed. (Privately owned)

240 (right). Appliqué quilt top, Album, c. 1830. 90" × 88". The many varieties of flowers incorporated in this design suggest it was made as a "memory" quilt, rather than intended as a gift. It is probably the work of one person. (Privately owned)

241 (above). Appliqué quilt, Whig Rose (variation), c. 1850, Pennsylvania (?). 93″ × 93″. A very strong pattern, carried out in sharp contrasts of red and orange-yellow flowers with green stems and leaves. (Henry Ford Museum)

242 (left). Appliqué quilt, Rose Wreath, c. 1850, possibly Midwest origin. 89½″ × 89½″. The design of the quilting enhances this simplified design in red and green. (Mr. and Mrs. Donald Morris)

243 (opposite, above), 243a (opposite, below). Appliqué quilt, Rose Wreath with Tulips, c. 1840, Pennsylvania. 88¼″ × 88″. Rose Wreath with Tulips became a popular variation on the simpler Rose Wreath pattern. The quilting is deep and in an all-over pattern, as can be seen in the detail on page 167. (Old Economy Village)

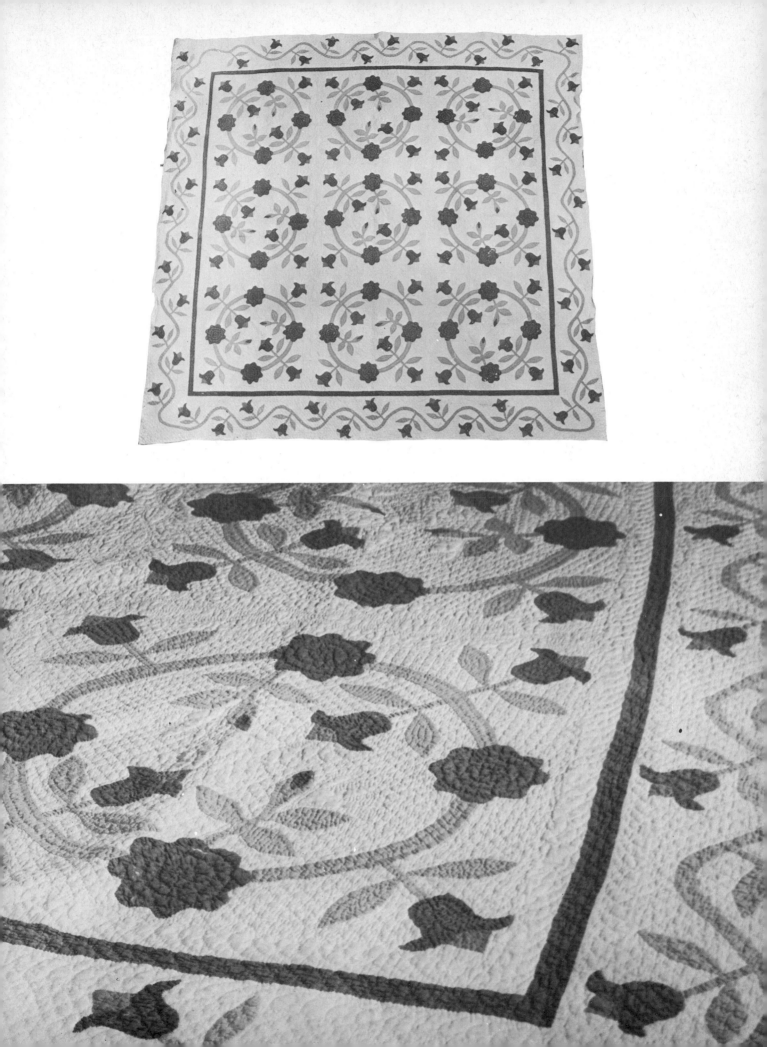

244 (above). Appliqué quilt, Roses and Buds, c. 1850, Vermont. 82½″ × 80½″. A fairly common design used in an unusual way—in squares instead of diamonds. The color is very lively: green, red, orange-yellow, and dark blue. Note that the designer had difficulty making her meandering border fit into the corners. (Mr. and Mrs. Leonard Balish)

245 (right). Appliqué quilt, Tulip (variation), c. 1875, Lancaster, Pennsylvania. 90″ × 80″. A typical Lancaster County design in the favored colors of the area, red and green. (Pennsylvania Farm Museum of Landis Valley)

246 (center). Appliqué and patchwork quilt, c. 1870, Pennsylvania. 100¾″ × 73½″. Fourteen vases of red-and-blue calico, each set in a large diamond-shaped block, contain bright flowers, fruit, and nine little birds. The way in which the vases have been set at different angles, together with the many types of flowers and fruit sprouting from them, and the random elements used in the border between the patchwork stars, all give the spread a charming, unstudied effect, rather as if one were walking in a garden. The quilting has been done in a flower-and-leaf design. Photograph courtesy John Gordon. (Privately owned)

247 (opposite, below left). Appliqué, Rose of Sharon, c. 1840, New England. 82″ × 80″. The use of extra flowers and buds fills each block of the design with a delicate light touch. (Henry Ford Museum)

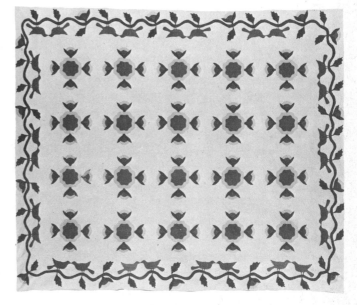

248 (above). Appliqué quilt, an Indiana
pattern, c. 1855. 87″ × 85″. The pattern, in blue, red,
yellow, and green, is a variation of Whig Rose. Eight
buds spring from each blossom, and the quilting
covers the entire spread. (Privately owned)

249 (below). Appliqué quilt, Whig Rose with Buds, c. 1850.
94″ × 78″. The handling of the bird-and-blossom border
contributes to the success of this strong Pennsylvania
German design. (Titus C. Geesey Collection,
Philadelphia Museum of Art)

250 (opposite). Appliqué and patchwork Remembrance quilt, c. 1841, Philadelphia. 125½″ × 119¼″. Information about the makers of this quilt is written in ink inside the rectangle with the appliqué frame at the center of the large wreath. The patchwork is made up of floral chintz and a calico. (Philadelphia Museum of Art)

251 (right), 251a (below). Appliqué quilt, c. 1831, Pennsylvania. 108″ × 108″. The chintz cutouts have been taken from three fabrics, one quite Oriental. The detail photograph below shows clearly the handsome stuffed quilting that covers the whole spread. (Old Economy Village)

252 (above). Appliqué quilt, chintz cutout, c. 1800. 96" × 90". The large size of this spread possibly indicates Southern handiwork. This type of spread is often called "Broderie Perse," since the chintz appliqués have been cut from an English chintz of Oriental design of c. 1770. (Ginsburg & Levy, Inc.)

253 (above), 253a (right). Broderie Perse coverlet, c. 1800, Pennsylvania. 120″ × 107″. Birds are featured in the cutouts from early English chintz. The beautiful trapunto quilting uses various flowers, grapes, and a large meandering border in the feather design. (Betty Sterling: Brainstorm Farm)

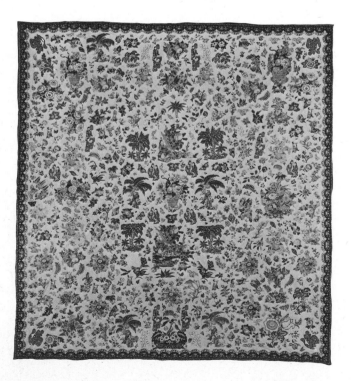

254 (left). Broderie Perse coverlet, c. 1800. 104″ × 98″. Nearly every square inch of this quilt is covered with large and small designs cut from an English chintz of Oriental design of c. 1750. (Ginsburg & Levy, Inc.)

255 (above). Appliqué quilt, c. 1799, made by Mrs. Charlotte Dabney of Dorchester, Maryland. 103″ × 98″. Wreaths, garlands, and the central motif are created by assembling cutouts from various printed cottons. The cutout flowers and leaves have been superimposed to create a realistic effect. (Cincinnati Art Museum)

256 (opposite, above left), 256a (left), 256b (opposite, above right). Appliqué quilt, c. 1830. 92″ × 92″. Another example of cutouts from English glazed chintz assembled and appliquéd to an American-made cotton backing. (Winterthur Museum)

257 (opposite, below) Appliqué quilt, Baltimore Friendship style, c. 1830. 105″ × 105″. Appliquéd and quilted and with some details made with pen and ink on the birds and leaves. Silk taffeta has been used in parts of the design. This is probably a "bride's quilt." (The Mount Vernon Ladies' Association of the Union)

258 (left). Appliqué crib quilt, c. 1810. 42½″ × 38½″. The designs were cut from chintz in large sections and appliquéd, hence the regularity of the design. The effect is unusual and very charming. (Privately owned)

259 (below). One of a group of corn-husk toys that depicts "The Quilting Bee," which was made by a Mrs. Cleveland. Many activities of life in early America are represented in this toy collection. (Essex Institute)

260 (above). Appliqué quilt, signed and dated "Sarah V. B. Quick 1844" inside the small wreath directly beneath the large vase of flowers. 98″ × 89½″. The quilt is composed of 106 small blocks and one large block onto which cutouts from eighteenth-century English chintz have been appliquéd. Some of the design elements have been repeated, giving a feeling of classic balance to the spread. The reader should apply a magnifying glass to this quilt to appreciate fully the incredible delicacy with which the chintz has been cut and appliquéd. Several of the other blocks carry signatures; therefore it would appear that the coverlet was worked by more than one person. The quilt is also unusual for being dated 1844, since most pieces of this type date from much earlier in the nineteenth century. (Privately owned)

261 (below), 261a (left). Appliqué quilt in a unique design. 83″ × 76″. Potted lilies on a small table in red, green, and chartreuse, comprise a new and different idea for a quilt, but one that is not very successful in terms of design. (Henry Ford Museum)

262 (left). Appliqué quilt block, Tulip pattern, c. 1830, Pennsylvania. Probably a beginner's piece. (Henry Ford Museum)

263 (opposite). Appliqué coverlet, c. 1790, Virginia. 110″ × 99″, excluding the fringe. This quilt descended in the family of Elizabeth Dandridge Henley, sister of Martha Washington. Several printed chintzes have been appliquéd in the form of flower baskets, festoons, and sprays. (The Mount Vernon Ladies' Association of the Union)

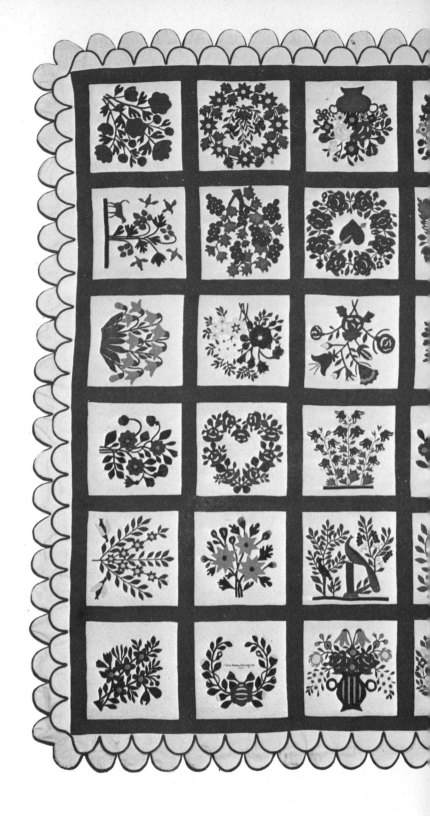

264 (center), 264a (left), 264b (opposite, right). Appliqué quilt, Album style, dated 1857 and inscribed Anna Putney Farrington. 100″ × 98″. Forty-two blocks, each with its bright individuality, are assembled into a splendid coverlet. The details give a good

idea of the workmanship involved. They are held in close harmony
by the red bands that frame each square. The double scalloped
border is another special feature of this noteworthy gift to a bride
or to a highly esteemed person. (Cora Ginsburg)

265 (above). Appliqué crib quilt, Album style, c. 1830. 32¾″ × 32¼″. Pink, green, red, and yellow compose the designs in this piece. Note the clasped hands surmounted with hearts. (Privately owned)

266 (below, left), 266a (below, right). Appliqué quilt, Indiana Wreath, made in Colorado in 1930 by Mrs. Charlotte Jane Whitehill. 90″ × 90″. Four calicoes and seven plain fabrics give an almost three-dimensional effect to this exquisite masterpiece, which is elaborately quilted in a feather design against a crisscross background. (Denver Art Museum)

267 (opposite, above right). Appliqué coverlet, c. 1835.
72″ × 54″. The quilting and trapunto work assume greater
importance in this spread than the appliqué design.
The macramé fringe makes an effective addition. (Ladies'
Hermitage Association)

268 (above). Appliqué coverlet, Sunflower, c. 1840.
86″ × 84″. All the pieces in this quilt are calico.
The flower design is in brown and white with red centers.
The border is delicately designed and relieves the weight
of the main design. (Privately owned)

271 (right). Appliqué quilt, Rose of Sharon (variation), c. 1850, Vermont. 79½″ × 78″. Repetition of the pattern, with two rows on the right facing two rows on the left, makes a stately design. Dark-red roses with light-green stems and leaves. (Privately owned)

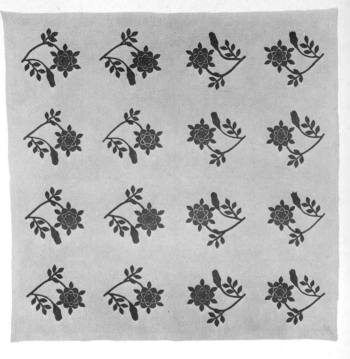

269 (left). Appliqué quilt, c. 1850, probably Pennsylvania. 94″ × 92″. A delightfully sprightly, elaborate design against a background quilted in a small waffle pattern. The colors of the swag border almost make it look as if it were composed of slices of watermelon! (Marguerite Riordan)

270 (left). Appliqué quilt, Whig Rose (variation), c. 1860, probably Pennsylvania. 92¾″ × 92½″. The yellow background emphasizes the power of this strongly conceived work. (Privately owned)

272 (above), 272a (opposite, below right). Appliqué quilt, unique Nosegay design, c. 1870. 91¼″ × 76½″. The bouquets of flowers have been created from folded fabric sewn together to form petals in an extraordinary three-dimensional *tour de force*. (Privately owned)

273 (above), 273a (below). Appliqué quilt, Peony, c. 1863, made by Mrs. Elizabeth Ann Cline of Knightstown, Indiana. 77" × 70". A variation of the Tulip pattern as it proceeded West. The real distinction of this spread is in the quilting. (Denver Art Museum)

275 (below), 275a (above). Appliqué quilt, Tulips in Vase, c. 1852, Pennsylvania German, made by Elizabeth Loehr. 85½" × 72¼". An original and restrained use of several typical Pennsylvania German motifs. (The Newark Museum)

274 (center). Appliqué quilt, Tulip (variation), c. 1835, Pennsylvania. 90" × 88". An ambitious and original design, showing a tendency on the part of the needlewoman not to leave well enough alone! The colors are red, green, and orange. (Henry Ford Museum)

276 (above). Appliqué quilt, design unidentified. 100″ × 88½″. Twenty identical blocks combine with a matching border to make a very successful coverlet. The delicacy of the diagonal stems provides good contrast to the simple flower (fruit?) forms. Photograph courtesy George Schoellkopf: The Peaceable Kingdom, Ltd. (Privately owned)

278 (below), 278a (above). Appliqué and patchwork quilt, Tulip, c. 1850. 98½″ × 90½″. The very delicate meandering border adds special interest to this familiar design in red and green. (George Schoellkopf: The Peaceable Kingdom, Ltd.)

277 (above). Appliqué and patchwork cradle quilt, Tulip (also called Virginia Lily or North Carolina Lily), c. 1820, Pennsylvania. 30¼″ × 23″. A diminutive use of this popular pattern. (Privately owned)

279 (left), 279a (below). Appliqué quilt, California Rose, made in 1931 by Mrs. Charlotte Jane Whitehill. 85″ × 85″ According to the quilt's creator, the pattern is "very old, from Kentucky." Some of the rose blossoms are made of red calico, and some of pink calico, and all are centered with yellow. The background is handsomely quilted in parallel diagonal lines combined with feather quilting. (Denver Art Museum)

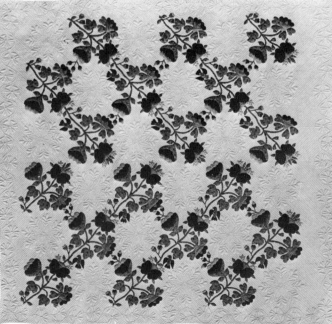

280 (above), 280a (opposite). Appliqué quilt, Martindale pattern, made in 1933 by Mrs. Charlotte Jane Whitehill. 84″ × 84″. A note about this quilt reads: "An old pattern from Aunt Martha Shaw, Carlyle, Ohio, about 1840, the Martindale family." The original of this quilt had come from Burlington, Vermont. The quilting is in the trapunto style. (Denver Art Museum)

281 (above). Appliqué quilt, Album, c. 1840. 101″ × 101″.
The repetition of some elements of the design in this
sixteen-block polychrome quilt suggests its having been
made by one person. Some of the blocks may have
been copied from another source. (Privately owned)

283 (below). Appliqué quilt, Princess Feather, c. 1810.
72″ × 68″. The quilting pattern cleverly echoes the
appliqué design. However, this design is perhaps more
overpowering than pleasing! (Henry Ford Museum)

282 (left). Appliqué quilt, Oak Leaf and Tulip, c. 1830.
92″ × 90″. The quilt is made entirely of plain red and blue
fabrics. The crossed stems of the tulips are interesting
and unusual, as is the tulip border. (Privately owned)

285 (opposite, below left). Appliqué quilt, Sunburst and
Rose of Sharon (variation), c. 1840, Pennsylvania.
82″ × 80¾″. An unusual approach to a conventional design
results in a strikingly successful pattern. Photograph courtesy
John Gordon. (Privately owned)

287 (opposite, below right). Appliqué quilt, Princess
Feather and Tulip, c. 1825, Pennsylvania. 83″ × 81″.
A successful variation of a typical design, bold in color.
(Privately owned)

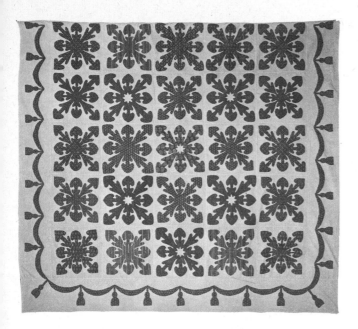

284 (left). Appliqué summer quilt, Double Hearts, signed and dated "A. I. Chance 1853." The particular interest of this strongly designed spread (called a "summer" quilt because the unquilted top is sewn to a plain cotton backing with no filling between) is the variation in the pattern derived from the several red calicoes used in the twenty-five blocks. Photograph courtesy Rhea Goodman: Quilt Gallery, Inc. (Privately owned)

286 (right). Appliqué quilt, Friendship, c. 1850, Akron, Ohio. 64″ × 56″. Signatures of many "friends" have been written in ink around the circular motifs as well as on the "petals" of the design. The colors are red on white. (Privately owned)

288 (left). Appliqué quilt, Whig Rose (variation), c. 1855, made by Mrs. Elizabeth Ann Cline of Knightstown, Indiana. 82″ × 73″. An unusual arrangement with the blossoms standing primly on stems sprouting from a neatly designed swag border. (Denver Art Museum)

290 (above). Appliqué quilt, Tulip, c. 1820, Pennsylvania. 88″ × 72″. An interesting quilt because of its very primitive quality. The heavy quilting in a broad, wavelike design echoes the naïve feeling of the piece. (Philadelphia Museum of Art)

289 (above). Appliqué quilt, unnamed design, c. 1835. 81½″ × 79¾″. An unusual combination of leaves and blossoms repeated sixteen times, creates an intense, successful quilt in red and green. The white center of each block is embroidered with a monogram. (Privately owned)

291 (left). Appliqué crib quilt, Ohio Rose (variation), c. 1850, Pennsylvania. 43½″ × 41½″. A successful, fresh arrangement of roses, buds, and leaves in red, orange, and yellow-green, rendered in the same scale one would find on a full-size spread. (Privately owned)

292 (right), 292a (below). Appliqué quilt, Poppy, 1920's. 93″ × 76½″. A well-designed and executed modern spread with blossoms in bright red and orange and leaves in dark green and light blue-green. The design realistically depicts a growing plant, with perhaps a touch of Art Nouveau feeling. (Rhea Goodman: Quilt Gallery, Inc.)

293 (opposite, above). Appliqué quilt, Tulip, c. 1840, Pennsylvania German. 89½″ × 85¼″. Strong design and strong colors here make a handsome, forceful statement of the quiltmaker's art in Pennsylvania. (Mr. and Mrs. Leonard Balish)

294 (opposite, below). Appliqué crib quilt, c. 1830, Pennsylvania. 41½″ × 41½″. A particularly striking use of the favorite Pennsylvania German heart motif. The pattern seems to have been cut and applied in large sections both in the central design and the border, which is quite unusual. (George Schoellkopf: The Peaceable Kingdom, Ltd.)

295 (above). Appliqué quilt, Coxcomb, c. 1870, Pennsylvania. 87″ × 85″. The border has been done in cable quilting and is well handled even in the corners. A tulip design is also included in the quilting. The four motifs are cut in one piece and appliquéd, an unusual feature in American quilts. Photograph courtesy George Schoellkopf: The Peaceable Kingdom, Ltd. (Privately owned)

296 (left). Appliqué quilt, Garden Island, c. 1840, Hawaii, made by Mrs. Mahikoa. 88½″ × 84″. Green on white, this quilt was designed to commemorate the founding of *The Garden Island*, Kauai's weekly newspaper. (Honolulu Academy of Arts)

297 (center). Appliqué quilt, *Pikake Lei* and Tuberose, c. 1950, Hawaii, made by Eleanor S. Anderson of the Bishop Museum staff. 84″ × 84″. This is an excellent modern example of the Hawaiian interpretation of American quilting. It is entirely quilted in concentric ridges conforming to the contours of the design. Photograph courtesy Honolulu Academy of Arts.

299 (opposite, below). Appliqué quilt, *Ke Kahi o Kaiulani*, c. 1840, Hawaii. 88½″ × 84″. A wine-red design on white, this is called "The Comb of Kaiulani." It combines an eight-rayed motif of combs and crowns with a surrounding *lei* of leaves. The waffle quilting covers the entire piece. (Honolulu Academy of Arts)

298 (right). Appliqué quilt, Grapevine, c. 1860, Hawaii. 84″ × 84″. The colors are red on white and the quilting has been done in diagonal parallel lines covering the pattern and the background. (Honolulu Academy of Arts)

300 (above), 300a (opposite, above). Appliqué quilt top, Album style, c. 1840, Ephrata, Pennsylvania. 94″ × 80″. The spread has been created from a plain red cotton. A wide variety of subjects has been included, with no particular "rhyme or reason" to them. A strong, graphic quilt. (Privately owned)

301 (below). Appliqué quilt, Album, inscribed "Harriet Knapp, Stamford, Connecticut, March A D 1854." 100½" × 87½". This "story" quilt was made to entertain children. Broad strips of plain red fabric divide the squares, in which prints and calicoes in blues, red, pink, green, and browns make the designs. The border is in green and red. (The Stamford Historical Society, Inc.)

302 (above). Appliqué quilt, Grapevine, c. 1860, Pennsylvania (?). 87″ × 87″. One of the most unusual appliqué and trapunto quilts to be preserved. The design is completely original, finely drawn, and expertly worked. The intertwining vines are tan, the grapes and bodies of the birds are grayish blue, and the flowers and birds' heads are red. (Privately owned)

304 (below). Appliqué quilt, c. 1845, made by Mrs. Priscilla Dodson of Cambridge, Maryland. 101½″ × 100″. The basket of flowers and the first and third borders are made of chintz cutouts. The grapevine and outermost border of swags are calico appliqué, all contributing to a varied yet very orderly design. (Philadelphia Museum of Art)

303 (left). Appliqué quilt, Oakleaf with Grapevine border, c. 1840. 90½″ × 90″. A carefully worked-out pattern of sixteen blocks. The border of tiny grapes, leaves, and tendrils is beautifully designed and executed. Though seemingly unrelated, the main elements of this spread work together to form a very handsome whole. The squarish form at the center of each block is orange with a bright green circle in the middle; the four dependent petals are red; the oak leaves green. In the border, the vine and tendrils are red with green grapes and leaves. (Mr. and Mrs. Leonard Balish)

305 (below), 305a (right). Appliqué quilt, Grape Vineyard, 1920's. 92″ × 74″. In this modern version of an old pattern the alternating blocks of grape quilting with no appliqué heightens the delicacy of this design of lavender grapes with green vine and leaves. (Rhea Goodman: Quilt Gallery, Inc.)

306 (above). Appliqué quilt, Album type, inscribed
"Mary Jane Naguy Feb 14, 1855." 82½″ × 81″. This
is probably best called a marriage quilt, since the designs
made by Mary Jane's twenty-four friends do not give much
of a clue as to the real occasion of the gift. (Privately owned)

307 (center), 307a (opposite, below), 307b (below).
Appliqué quilt, Rose of Sharon, c. 1840, probably
Pennsylvania. 82″ × 68″. A splendid example of folk art
in quilting, this elaborate and colorful spread boasts several
kinds of flowers, birds, and animals, as well as Adam and Eve
with the serpent entwined in a calico tree. A most engaging
piece. (Privately owned)

309 (right), 309a (below), 309b (right). Appliqué unquilted Friendship coverlet, c. 1846, Baltimore. 88″ × 88″. Nearly all the blocks in this very detailed quilt are signed and dated. It is in use at the Carroll Mansion in Baltimore. (The Peale Museum)

308 (left). Appliqué Album quilt, Remembrance type, c. 1840, probably Baltimore. 88¼″ × 87½″. This is obviously the work of one person, who apparently created the spread to record her delight in flowers, some of them, perhaps, growing in her own garden. The colors are varied and natural, including reds, blues, pinks, greens, and bright orange. The designs are strong and handsome. (Mr. and Mrs. Leonard Balish)

310 (opposite). Appliqué and patchwork Friendship quilt, dated 1860. 92½″ × 75½″. A label sewn to the quilt reads: "This quilt was made by Mrs. Newton Darrow and friends in 1860. Property of Reverend and Mrs. E. W. Darrow." (Privately owned)

311 (above), 311a (below), 311b (center). Appliqué quilt, Princess Feather, c. 1820. 71½″ × 69″. This design became popular early and was carried across the country. It was not a simple form to cut and appliqué. The colors suggest that this example was made in Pennsylvania. The lining of this quilt, in the same bold colors as the top, is illustrated at the right. It is made of patchwork and inescapably reminds one of the modern paintings by Piet Mondrian (1872–1944). The quilt was undoubtedly intended to be reversible. Photograph courtesy George Schoellkopf: The Peaceable Kingdom, Ltd. (Rhea Goodman: Quilt Gallery, Inc.)

312 (below). Appliqué quilt, Tulip, modern, Pennsylvania. 87″ × 86½″. Tulips and leaves sprouting from the tulips create a pinwheel design in fresh, springlike colors that is very pleasant. The bending tulips in the border suggest a windy day. Photograph courtesy George Schoellkopf: The Peaceable Kingdom, Ltd. (Privately owned)

313 (bottom). Appliqué quilt, Princess Feather (variation), c. 1825, Pennsylvania German. 87½″ × 87″. The feather-quilted border holds this strong pattern together in a way most quilts of this design fail. The design is red and green on an orange ground. (Philadelphia Museum of Art)

314 (right), 314a (above). Detail of an appliqué quilt, probably late nineteenth century. Quite touching in its simplicity, this is a primitive attempt at needlework illustrations. An Indian hunts a stag, while two others are apparently sneaking up on the man with a gun, who is identified in embroidery as Buffalo Bill. In the further detail above we see the Christmas angel saying (again in embroidery) to the hatted shepherd, "Behold, I bring you glad tidings of great joy," while the star is labeled, "The star which hovers over Bethlehem." (Henry Ford Museum)

315 (left), 315a (above). Appliqué quilt, Biscuit pattern, c. 1820, New England, made by Miss P. Reynolds. A unique feature of this coverlet is the raised, bisquit-like frame separating the blocks the designer has named in sequence from the upper left: "The Lily-of-the-Valley; The Compass; The Wanderer's Path in the Wilderness; The Tree of Paradise; Cactus Blossom; Bird of Paradise; The Royal Japanese Vase; The Blazing Star; The Star of Bethlehem; Old Folks at Home to Dinner; Old Log Cabin, Spruce, Two Stumps; The Rose of Sharon; The Pineapple; Dog Days, Stars, Sun, and the Covenant; June Lip; Evening Star." (Bedford Historical Society)

316 (below), 316a (right). Appliqué quilt, c. 1895, made by Mrs. Harriet Powers of Athens, Georgia. 105″ × 69″. Mrs. Powers has thoughtfully identified for posterity the scenes depicted in her fascinating pictorial quilt. Left to right, and top to bottom: "Job Praying for His Enemies; The Dark Day of May 19, 1780; The Serpent Lifted Up by Moses; Adam and Eve in the Garden; John Baptising Christ; Jonah Casted Overboard; God Created Two of Every Kind, Male and Female; The Falling of the Stars, November 13, 1833; Two of Every Kind of Animals; The Angels of Wrath and the Seven Vials; Cold Thursday, February 10, 1895—a Man Frozen at His Jug of Liquor; The Red Light Night of 1846; Rich People Were Taught Nothing of God; The Creation of Animals Continued; The Crucifixion of Christ Between Two Thieves—the Blood and Water Run from His Right Side." (Museum of Fine Arts, Boston; Bequest of Maxim Karolik)

317 (opposite). Appliqué and patchwork quilt, House, c. 1875. 80″ × 65″. A naïve version of the House pattern, this coverlet gains its striking effect from the many colorful prints used and their interaction with the bright-yellow background. (Rhea Goodman: Quilt Gallery, Inc.)

318 (above, right), 318a (above). Appliqué quilt, House, c. 1875. 82″ × 79″. We admire in this spread the strong color, the regularity of the design, and the textural interest created by the play of the plain fabric against the striped ticking, as seen in the detail. (Rhea Goodman: Quilt Gallery, Inc.)

319 (below, right). Appliqué bedcover, inscribed "Christmas, 1881." 92″ × 80″. The subject matter in bright polychrome and inscription make it obvious this piece was made to delight a child. Jack and Jill draw their pail of water at top right; Gulliver has been securely fastened at bottom left; and Jack Sprat and his wife appear to be dancing under the kite! (Barbara Johnson)

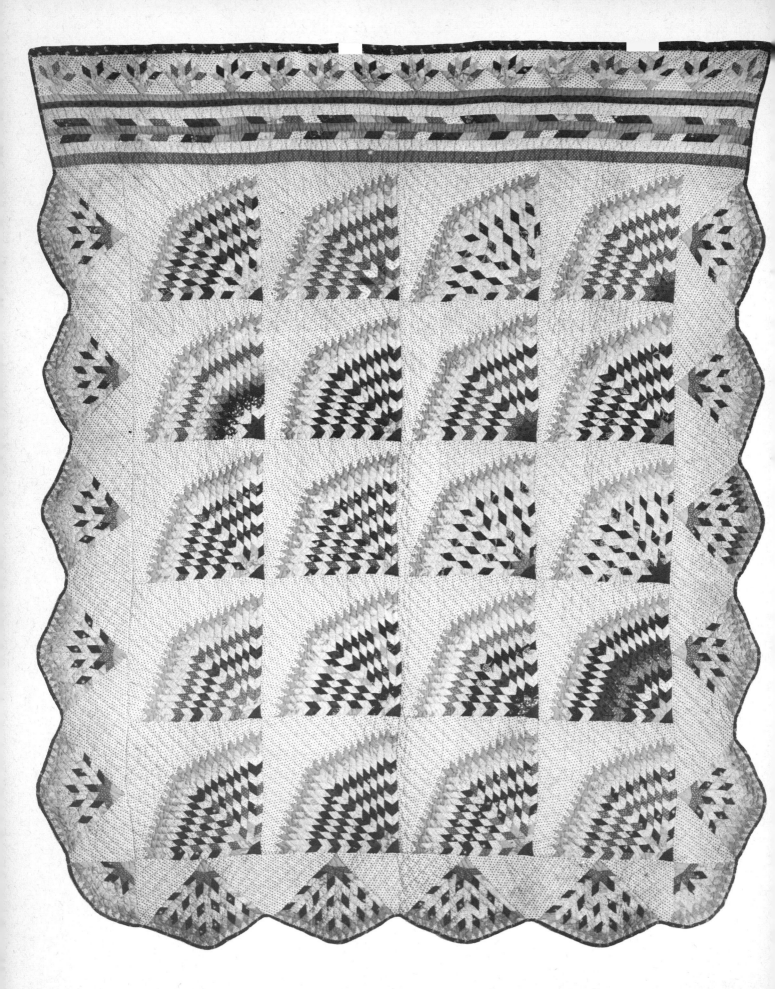

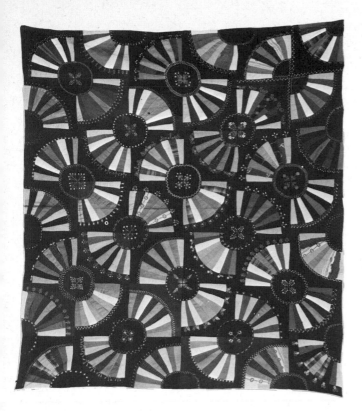

320 (opposite). Appliqué "throw," Fan, c. 1900. 92″ × 80″.
Made of wools joined with superb examples of feather-
stitching. (Henry Ford Museum)

321 (left). Appliqué and patchwork throw, c. 1880.
76″ × 63″. Patchwork has been used to create the Victorian
fan pattern embellished with fancy stitching.
(Henry Ford Museum)

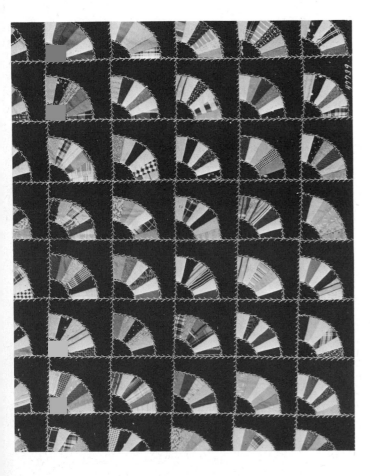

322 (left). Appliqué throw, c. 1900. 74″ × 60″. Nearly
every woman in America made one of these from her velvet
and silk remnants. The simplest featherstitch was all
she needed to learn from her copy of "*Peterson's.*"
(Henry Ford Museum)

323 (above). Appliqué throw, Japanese Fan, c. 1900.
62½″ × 62½″. Elaborate embroidery and stitching combines
with patterned silks in light and dark colors to make a very
elegant and Oriental-looking version of the Fan design.
(Privately owned)

324 (opposite, above). Appliqué quilt, Album, c. 1790, made by Cynthia Arsworth of Baltimore. 94½″ × 92″. There is great variety of color and much embroidery in this very floral quilt. (Philadelphia Museum of Art)

325 (opposite, below). Appliqué quilt top, Album, c. 1820. 103″ × 84″. This quilt is probably the work of several people. The designs are varied and the workmanship shows several levels of experience. (Henry Ford Museum)

326 (above). Appliqué coverlet, made in 1870 by Hannah Riddle of Woolwich, Maine. 77½″ × 76″. Made of felt with strips of blue velvet at the top and bottom, this is a gigantic piece of work and a beautiful example of design and color working together, in this instance producing almost a stained-glass effect. There is no apparent theme for the multitude of designs—just Mrs. Riddle's creative imagination running riot. This coverlet won First Prize at the Woolwich Fair in 1870. Photograph courtesy Ryther House Gallery. (Privately owned)

327 (above), 327a (right). Appliqué quilt, 1938, Ohio.
91″ × 79″. This extraordinary "painting" is inscribed with
the dates "1788–1938" on the frame, and it was apparently
created to memorialize the treaty made with the Indians
on the banks of the Marietta River in Ohio. Note how the
needleworker has used her quilting to depict so expertly
cloud forms, the foliage and bark of the trees, the stockade,
the water, and many other fascinating details, including the
final touch—the wood grain of the painting's frame.
(Privately owned)

328 (above). "The Hudson River Quilt." 96½″ × 79¾″. A shared interest in New York's Hudson River and a concern for its beauty prompted twenty-nine needleworkers to join, at her invitation, Irene Preston Miller of Croton-on-Hudson, New York, to create this unique example of appliqué quilting. Work on it was started in June 1969, and the quilt was completed in May 1972. Funds raised by the quilt will go toward the preservation of the Hudson River. Among the scenes depicted in the thirty panels are the source of the Hudson at Lake Tear of the Clouds, the Capitol at Albany, the Mid-Hudson Bridge at Poughkeepsie, Croton Point, the Hudson River Museum in Yonkers, the George Washington Bridge with the Little Red Lighthouse beneath, Carl Carmer's Octagon House in Irvington, the Manhattan Skyline, and New York Harbor. Photograph courtesy Irene Preston Miller.

THE OVERSHOT COVERLET

The four main types of American coverlets are Overshot, Double Weave, Summer and Winter, and Jacquard. The earliest coverlets were probably brought from Europe as household goods, and these eventually had to be replaced. Almost every family possessed a small four-harness loom (as well as coverlet patterns or "drafts"), either brought from Europe or fashioned in America of hand-hewn logs; and the girls in the family had been taught to spin the linen and wool that made the warp and weft of the coverlets. Thus coverlets were one of the early forms of home weaving. However, we do not have examples of seventeenth- and early eighteenth-century coverlets that we can date to those periods with certainty, for names and dates were not used on these early coverlets. Studies of several collections seem to indicate that most of the earliest Overshot coverlets originated in New York.

We are fortunate in that three books of coverlet patterns or drafts survive in museum collections. Although all are in poor condition, they are still clearly usable. One of two such books in the collection of the Philadelphia Museum of Art belonged to John Landes, one of a family of Mennonite weavers who traveled by horse and cart from farm to farm, setting up shop and weaving whatever the household needed at the time. There are seventy-seven patterns in this book.

The pattern book owned by the Henry Ford Museum belonged to the "Misses Muenscher," of Somerset Avenue, Taunton, Massachusetts. The young women entitled their book *Ancient Patterns for Weaving Handloom Bed Covers: Age from 100 to 150 years* (but there is no date recorded in the book!). It contains seven patterns shown in color. These drafts for threading a loom were the "recipe book" for another German family and are written on four bars representing the four frames or harnesses of the loom.

For an Overshot coverlet, the warp usually consisted of a natural-color linen thread and the weft was a wool homespun in a color, or shades of one color. Later examples of Overshot coverlets were made with a colored warp as well as multicolored wefts. The patterns could be combinations of stripes, squares, diamonds, and a weft "float" in color over the tabby or plain weave of the background. In this type the "skips" or floats of wool lie on top of the linen and so were often damaged and broken in use. The Overshot coverlet was always seamed through the middle, and exact matching of the design was often disregarded. To the critical eye, therefore, the design would appear distracting. In the Southern states, however, it was believed that such a break in a straight line would deflect evil spirits and insure good luck for the user of the spread.

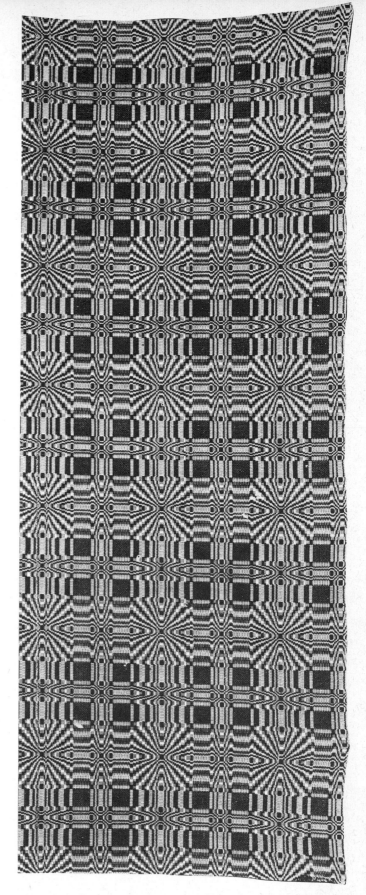

329 (opposite). Detail of an Overshot coverlet, Snail's Trail, c. 1800. This was woven by slaves on one of the Lovelace Plantations near LaGrange, Georgia. (The Old Slave Mart Museum)

330 (above). Overshot coverlet, Sunrise (variation), c. 1830. Indigo-blue and white. 94½″ × 83½″. (Privately owned)

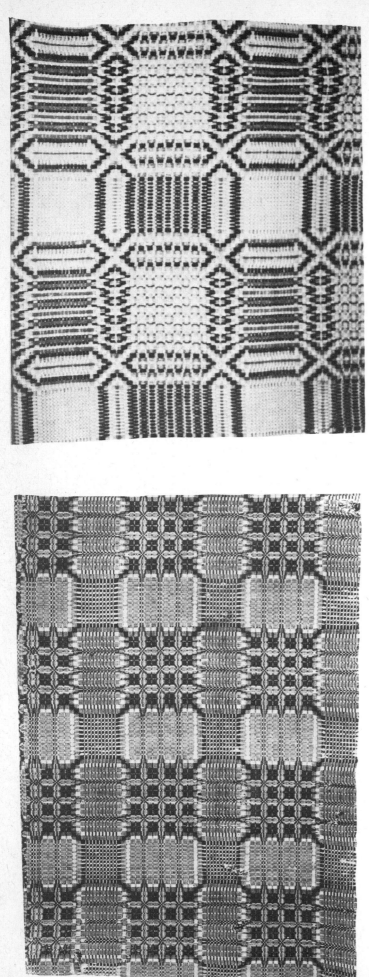

331 (left). Detail of an Overshot coverlet, Pine Bloom, c. 1810, Bedford County, Tennessee. 102″ × 79½″. Woven in three 26″ strips and whipped carefully together. It is in red and blue on creamy white. (Oaklands Association, Inc.)

332 (below, left). Detail of an Overshot coverlet, Sea Star, c. 1820. 93¼″ × 68″. Indigo-blue and coral wool on natural cotton warp. (Philadelphia Museum of Art)

333 (below). Overshot coverlet, Frenchman's Fancy, c. 1820. 196″ × 44″. This is a rare example of weaving just as it was removed from the loom—twice as long and half as wide as the finished coverlet it would be made into by cutting the woven length in half and then sewing the two pieces together to form a seam down the middle. Loops in the weft are uncut as seen in this illustration, but they were to become side fringe when the coverlet was completed. (Henry Ford Museum)

334 (above). Detail of an Overshot coverlet, Cross and Diamonds, c. 1830. 88″ × 67″. The weft is red, warp is natural. Photographed from the wrong side. (Philadelphia Museum of Art)

335 (above, right). Detail of an Overshot coverlet, Olive Leaf, c. 1820. 86½″ × 43¼″. Red and blue design with white cotton warp. (Philadelphia Museum of Art)

336 (right). Detail of an Overshot coverlet, Lover's Chain (variation), c. 1850. 90″ × 79″. Black and rust wool on natural cotton warp, three widths sewn together. (Philadelphia Museum of Art)

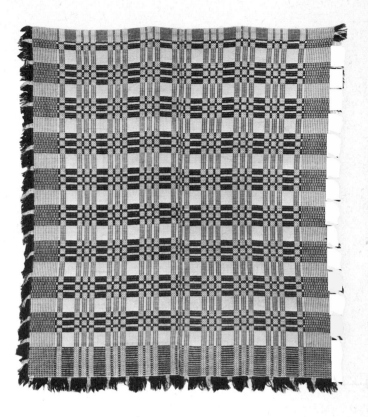

337 (opposite, above). Overshot coverlet, Twenty-four States, c. 1830. 93″ × 67″. Initialed "C M." Red and blue with white warp, fringe on one end. (Faye and Don Walters)

338 (opposite, below). Overshot blanket, c. 1800, New England. Many varieties of plaids, such as this example in red, white, and dark blue, were made in several colors from natural dyes on the ordinary household loom of two or four harnesses. Such plaids were termed "blanket weave," which was sometimes a plain weave, but more usually a twill weave. (Privately owned)

339 (center). Overshot coverlet, Fox's Chase (variation), c. 1830. 90″ × 66″. The original blue-green color of the square blocks, as seen in the left half of the coverlet, has changed on the right side into an effective variety of colors, probably due to uneven fading through the years, in turn due, perhaps, to a less-than-expert job of wool dyeing when the piece was first made. (Privately owned)

340 (above). Overshot coverlet, Nine Snowballs, c. 1840. 82″ × 66″. Enriched by three striking colors, blue, red, and gold against the creamy warp, this is an outstanding coverlet, with applied fringe on three sides, and a hemmed top. (Privately owned)

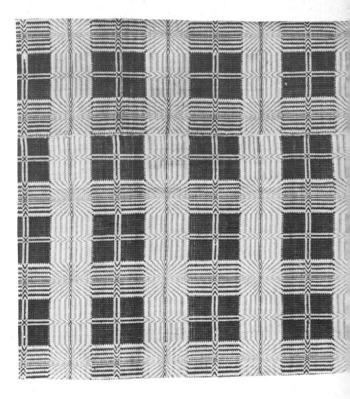

341 (left). Overshot coverlet, Double Chariot Wheels, c. 1830. A fragment only. Red, green, and gold wool on white cotton warp. (Henry Ford Museum)

342 (left), 342a (opposite). Overshot coverlet, Dog Tracks, c. 1838. 78½″ × 68″. Natural butternut-dyed weft and white warp. (The Stamford Historical Society, Inc.)

343 (above). Detail of an Overshot coverlet, Sunrise and Windows, c. 1840. 89″ × 84″. Red and green wool on white warp. (Henry Ford Museum)

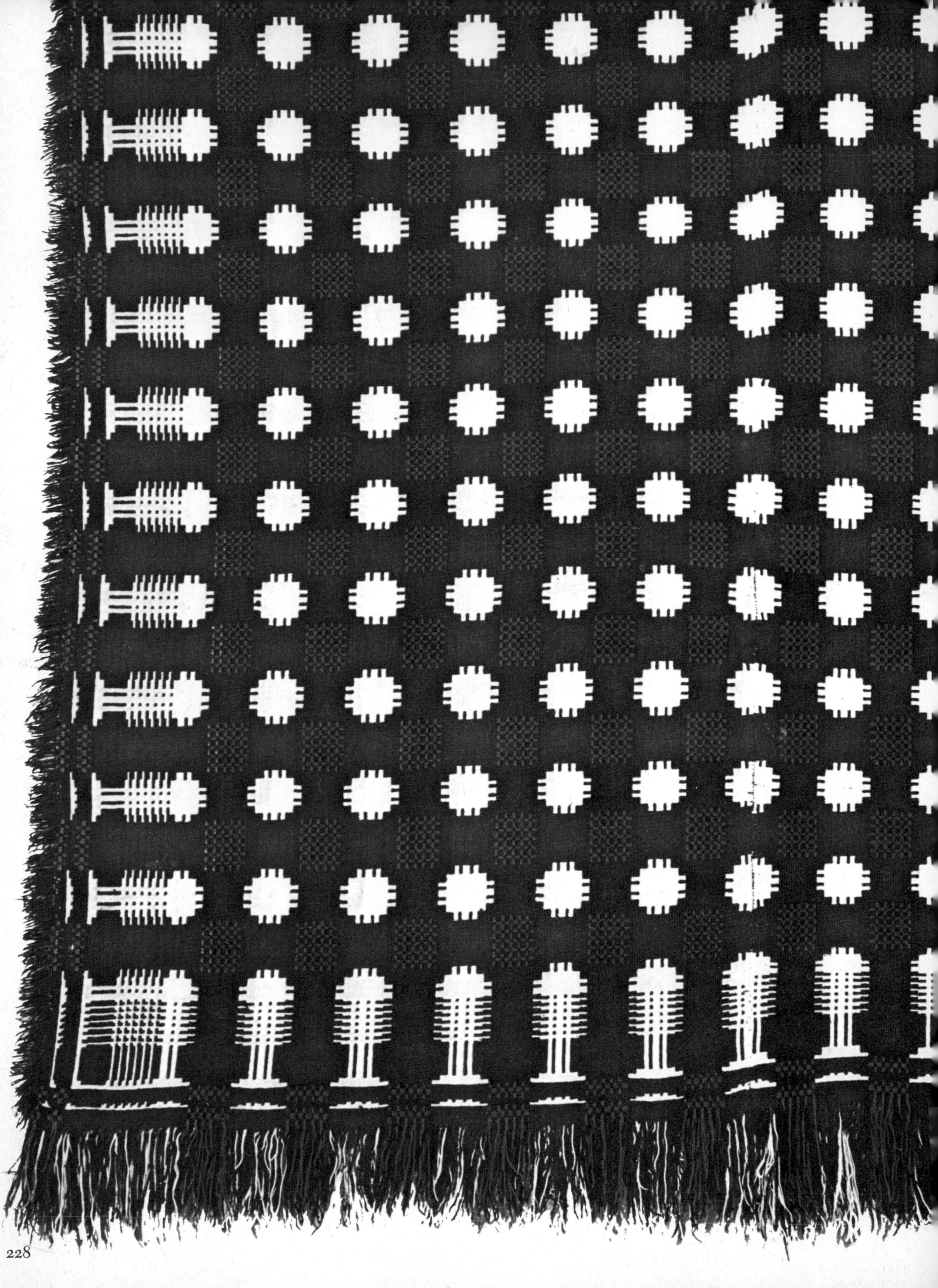

THE DOUBLE WEAVE COVERLET

The patterns used in Double Weave coverlets were principally geometric, and thus similar in style to the Overshot and Summer and Winter types. However, the Double Weave coverlets were constructed so that *two* "webs" or warps joined in such a way that the reverse side of the coverlet was a mirror image of the front. Thus the front would show a dark design on a light ground, and the back a light design on a dark ground. The space between the front and back can actually be separated by pulling them apart with the fingers, as one can do with a pocket. Many modern upholstery fabrics are woven in the same way, and are called "pocket-weave."

The Double Weave style has generally been thought to cover the period from 1725 to 1825, but surviving examples are all from the end of this period. These spreads were woven in narrow widths and seamed through the middle, since forty inches was the average distance a weaver could throw his shuttle.

In the collection of the New York State Historical Association in Cooperstown is the account book kept by James Alexander, a weaver in Little Britain, Orange County, New York. Discovered in 1956, this book gives some substantiation to an early date for the introduction of Double Weave coverlets in America.

James Alexander was born of Scottish parents in Belfast, Ireland, but he came to New York when he was twenty-eight and became a farmer-weaver. He was able to hire help for his loom on a day-to-day basis, and turned out a great deal of exceptional work. His assistants were usually English or Scottish and had passed the rigorous tests of the weavers' guild. The entries in the record book show that Alexander was equipped to weave linen damask for the table and Double Weave carpets and coverlets. His earliest entry for a woven coverlet is 1805, the earliest date yet recorded for the Double Weave style. Between 1816 and 1824 he produced great numbers of complicated types of Double Weave carpets and coverlets, and lists orders for 247 coverlets with the names to be woven into the corners. In 1818 Alexander advertised that he was in the weaving business: "Diaper and Damask, Diaper, of the Completest European patterns from 1 to 2½ yards wide, Flowered Carpets, Carpet Coverlids, full-breadth or half, as suit the owners, Counterpanes, of any pattern or size . . ." Several of these items would have required a loom twice the size of the regular loom and a "fly shuttle" or two assistants sitting at the sides of of the loom to throw the shuttle between them. Alexander's coverlet drafts are not drawn or listed in his account books.

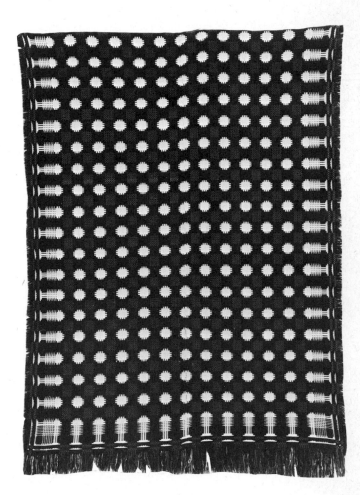

344 (above, right), 344a (opposite). Double Weave coverlet, Snowball with Pine Tree border, c. 1820. 90″ × 70″. Red and blue wool on white warp. The color plate on the opposite page clearly illustrates the border motif consisting of three "pine trees" clumped together into one decorative unit. (Privately owned)

Ancient Patterns
for weaving
Hand-loom Bed-covers.
Age from 100 to 150 years.

Misses Muenscher.
Somerset Avenue.
Taunton. Mass.

347 (below). One of the pages from the draft book compiled by the Misses Muenscher. All the designs are in watercolor—black combined with two or three other colors. The zeros and the check marks resemble music notations, but are an aid for warping the loom. (Henry Ford Museum)

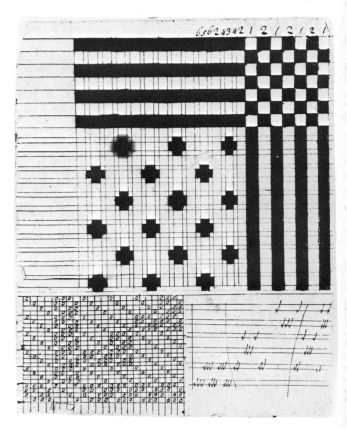

345 (above). Title page from a small book of "drafts," or weaving patterns, from Taunton, Massachusetts. Since there is no date on this notebook, it is probable that it was compiled some years after the popularity of the coverlet, and was intended to stand as a record for posterity. (Henry Ford Museum)

346 (below). A series of drafts noted down by a weaver from North Carolina. An experienced weaver of today would have no difficulty in interpreting these notations in order to set his or her own loom to create the pattern described in these jottings. (Ginsburg & Levy, Inc.)

348 (above). One of seventy-seven weaving designs from the notebooks of John
Landes, c. 1800. Landes was a Pennsylvania German weaver who worked in the late
eighteenth century and the first quarter of the nineteenth. The majority of the
drawings are in black and white, but some have been rendered in three colors.
The directions are in German. Pattern No. 16, shown here, is a variation of Lover's
Knot or Whig Rose. (Philadelphia Museum of Art)

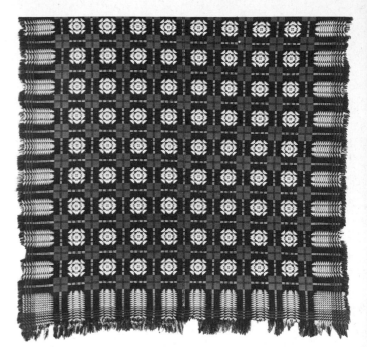

351 (above). Double Weave coverlet, Snowflake with Pine Tree border, 1820. 81″ × 73¼″. Two shades of blue with white warp. (Henry Ford Museum)

349 (above). Detail of a Double Weave coverlet, Lover's Knot (variation), with Cruciform border, c. 1820. 90½″ × 84½″. Red and indigo wool and white warp. Probably Pennsylvania German. This coverlet was owned by the wife of John Morton, a signer of the Declaration of Independence. (Philadelphia Museum of Art)

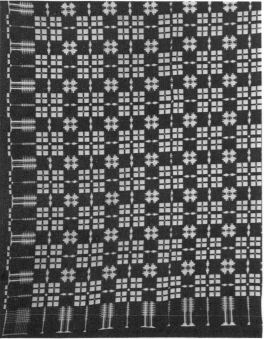

350 (left). Detail of a Double Weave coverlet, Snowflake and Windows, c. 1810. 79½″ × 78½″. Brick-red and dark blue. (Privately owned).

352 (above). Double Weave coverlet, pattern unidentified, Pine Tree border, c. 1820. 83″ × 72¾″. Coral red and dark blue on white warp. (Allan L. Daniel)

353 (below). Double Weave coverlet, pattern unidentified, Pine Tree border, c. 1820. 96″ × 81½″. Red-orange and blue on white warp with fringe on three sides. (Privately owned)

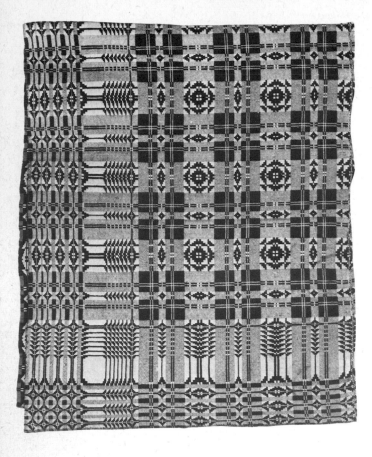

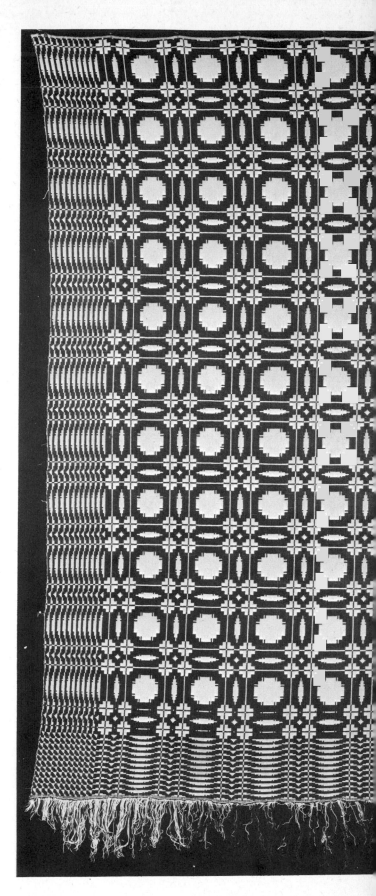

354 (above). Detail of a Double Weave coverlet, Snowflake with Pine Tree border, c. 1820. 82″ × 64″. Brick-red and blue on white warp. (Privately owned)

355 (center). Double Weave coverlet, Snowball, c. 1830. 90″ × 76½″. Green wool on cream warp. (Privately owned)

356 (opposite, above). Double Weave coverlet, Snowflake and Tile pattern, c. 1830. 100″ × 78″. Navy and white. (Privately owned)

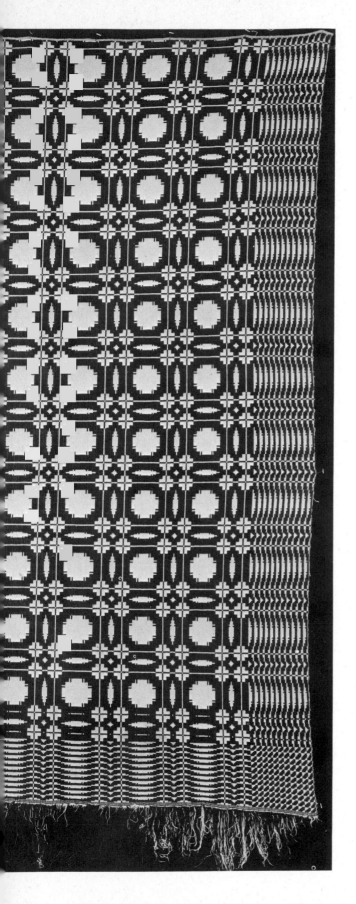

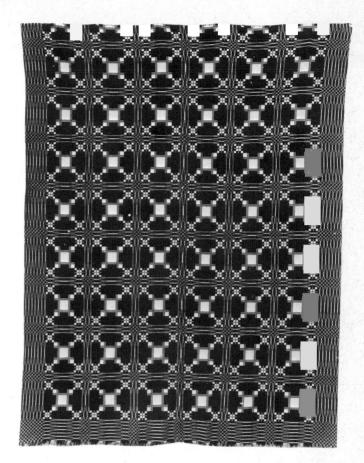

357 (right). Detail of a Double Weave coverlet, Single Snowball with Pine Tree border, c. 1830. 79″ × 67″. Blue and white. (Henry Ford Museum)

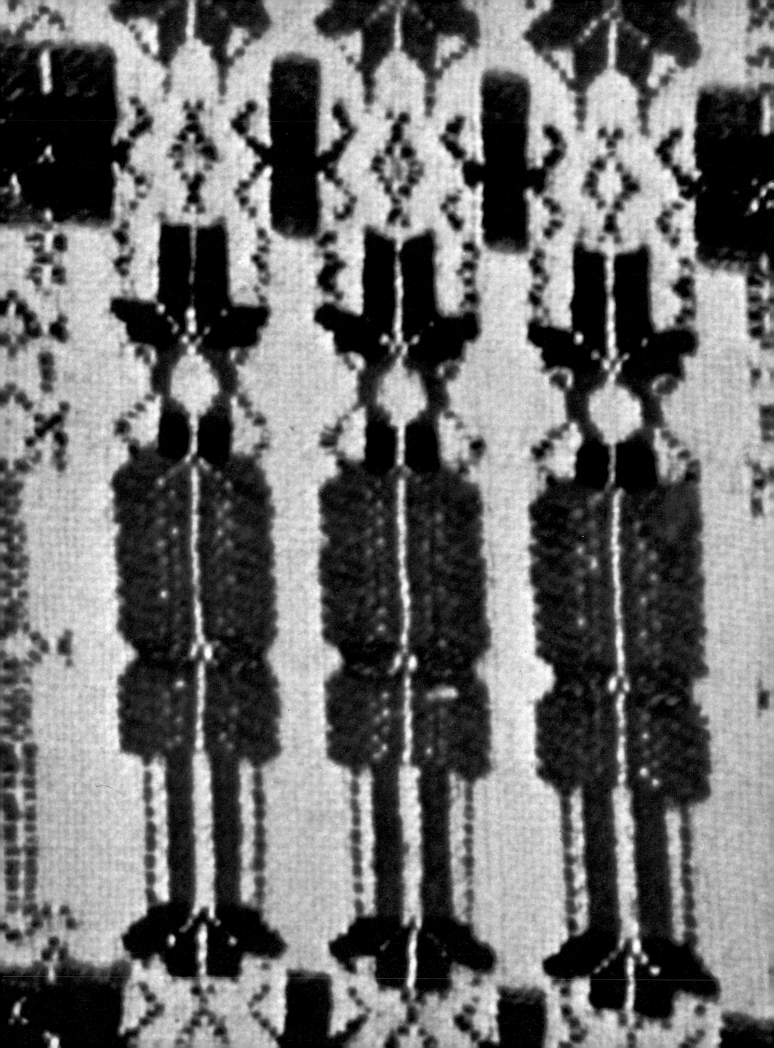

THE SUMMER
AND WINTER COVERLET

This type of double-faced coverlet (in which the weaving of the back is the reverse of that on the front) seems to have originated in America. It was possible to make such a coverlet on a four-harness loom, although six or eight harnesses allowed more variety in the pattern. The Summer and Winter coverlet shows a desire to elaborate on the simple geometric style of the Overshot type. It was not a heavy coverlet, and undoubtedly its name was prompted by the fact it could be used in all seasons.

Summer and Winter coverlets were probably made in Pennsylvania, for there was an influx of professional weavers from Germany who might possibly have created all the examples that remain. In this style the pattern thread or weft is closely interwoven with the warp, and there are no long skips as in the Overshot style. A flatter pattern is thus created, but the pattern is still basically geometrical.

An unusual example of the Summer and Winter style in the Henry Ford Museum (figure 367) has a most interesting border treatment, resembling drawn work, in three rows around three sides of the spread. The delicate, lacelike quality of this edging has resulted in its becoming very shabby, but it remains an unusual and attractive specimen.

358 (below), 358a (opposite). Details of a Summer and Winter coverlet, Nine Star with Soldier (?) border, c. 1830. 99½″ × 76½″. Red and blue on a cream warp. This coverlet is a most unusual example because of the figures, which may well represent soldiers, that have been woven into the border. (Privately owned)

360 (right). Summer and Winter coverlet, Star and Diamond, c. 1820. 102″ × 84″. A very popular pattern in red-orange, dark blue, and cream. (George Schoellkopf: The Peaceable Kingdom, Ltd.)

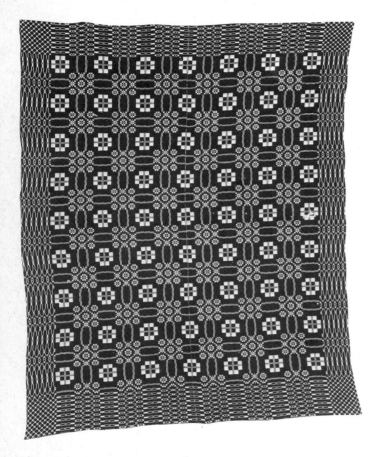

359 (above). Summer and Winter coverlet, Lover's Knot (variation). 92¾″ × 76½″. Blue on white. Woven in 1789 by Esther Hoyt of Stamford, Connecticut. (The Stamford Historical Society, Inc.)

361 (right). Detail of a coverlet of unnamed pattern, c. 1840. 92½″ × 80½″. Light blue, dark blue, and red-orange. The Colonial Coverlet Guild of America owns nothing close to this design. (Privately owned)

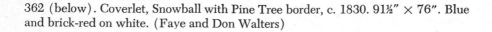
362 (below). Coverlet, Snowball with Pine Tree border, c. 1830. 91½" × 76". Blue and brick-red on white. (Faye and Don Walters)

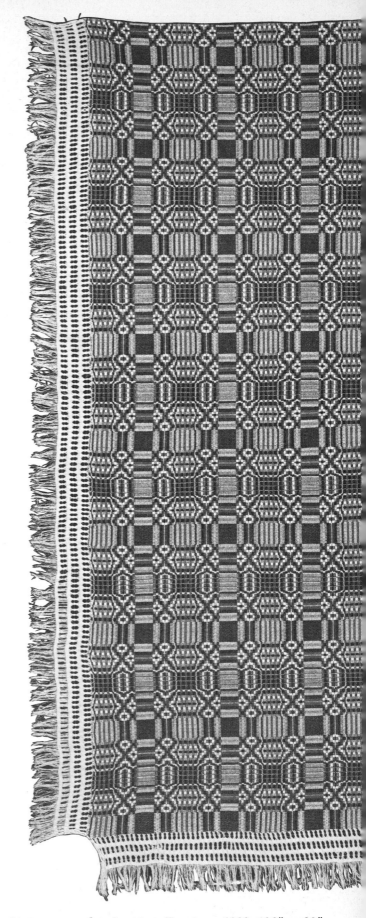

363 (above). Summer and Winter coverlet, Rose (variation), c. 1830. 104¾″ × 89″. Red, blue, and green. (Privately owned)

364 (below). Summer and Winter coverlet, Sixteen Snowballs, c. 1830. 87½″ × 83½″. Red and blue on white warp. (Privately owned)

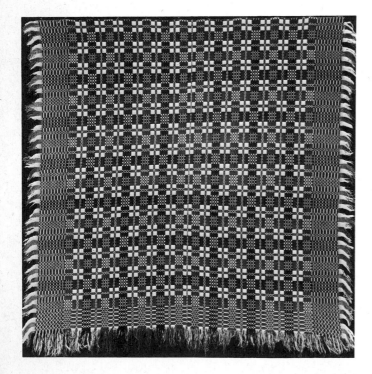

365 (center). Summer and Winter coverlet, American Beauty, c. 1830. 106″ × 90″. Brick-red, black, and natural. It is uncommon to find a coverlet with the original fringe remaining in such good condition. In this example the delicate fringe was woven separately on another loom from the thread of the warp and then sewn to the three sides of the coverlet. (Privately owned)

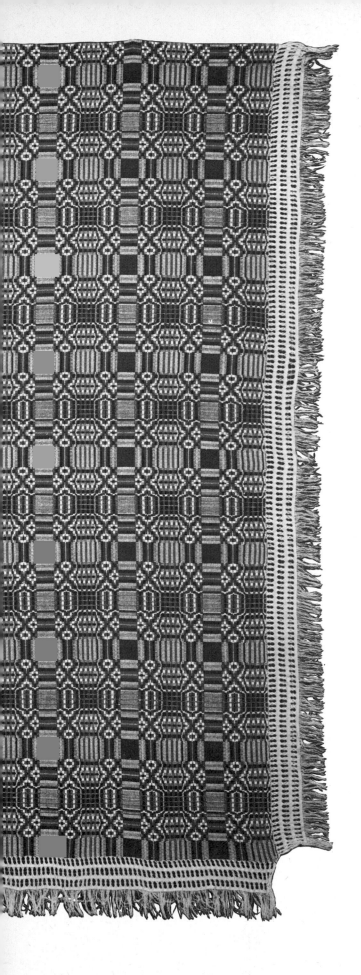

366 (above). Detail of a Summer and Winter coverlet, Chariot Wheels, c. 1830. 89″ × 70″. (Privately owned)

367 (below). Summer and Winter coverlet, Mosaics, c. 1810. 105″ × 99″. Blue and white. The borders have been specially woven to represent hemstitching or drawn work by inserting bands of reed during the weaving. (Henry Ford Museum)

COVERLET TITLES

THE FOLLOWING LIST CON-
TAINS THE NAMES OF COVER-
LETS MADE IN THE OVERSHOT,
DOUBLE WEAVE, AND SUMMER
AND WINTER STYLES.

FLOWERY, LEAFY, AND POETIC
NAMES

Blooming Flower
Catalpa Flower
China Leaves
Cluster of Vines
Dogwood Blossom (Ky. and Tenn.)
Dogwood Rose
Double Rose
Fading Leaf
Fig Leaf
Flower of the Mountain (N.C.)
Flowers of Canaan
Flowers of Edinboro (Ky. and Tenn.)
Flowers of Lebanon (Mass.)
Flowery Plains (Tenn.)
Flowery Vine
Folding Leaf
Four Snowballs
Governor's Garden
Granny's Garden (Ky.)
Hickory Leaf
Holly Leaf
Indiana Frame Rose (N.C.)
Islands of the Sea (Conn.)
Kentucky Snowballs (Ky.)
King's Flower (Ky. and N.C.)
King's Garden (Me.)
Laurel Blossom
Leaf and Snowball
Lemon Leaf (Ky.)
Lily of the Valley (N.C.)
Lily of the West
Magnolia (Tenn.)
Mountain Flower (Tenn.)
Mountain Rose
Nine Snowballs
Old Roads (W. Va.)
Olive Leaf
Orange Trees
Pansies and Roses in the Wilderness
Path of the Sunbeam (Me.)
Peony Leaf (Va.)
Pine Bloom (Ky.)
Pine Burr
Pine Top
Piney Rose (N.C.)
Pomegranate
Primrose (Conn., 1813)
Primrose and Diamonds
Red Rose (Va.)

Reed Leaf
Rose and Blossoms
Rose and Compass
Rose and Diamonds
Rosebud
Rose in Bloom
Rose in Blossom
Rose in the Garden (N.C.)
Rose in the Valley
Rose in the Wilderness (Ky.)
Rose Leaf and Bud
Rose of Sharon (Ky.)
Rose of the Valley
Roses and Pinies in the Wilderness
Rose Walk (Sweden)
Rosy Walk
Shamrock (Tenn.)
Single Snowballs
Sixteen Snowballs
Snowball and Dewdrop
Snowball and Leaf
Snowballs
Snow Drop
Spring Flower
Sun Flower
Sunrise on the Walls of Troy
Trailing Vine (Ky. and Tenn.)
Twining Vine (Ky.)
Wandering Vine
Wide World's Wonder
Winding Vine (Ky. and Tenn.)
Wonder of the Forest (Va.)
World's Wonder (Ky.)
Wreaths and Roses (Tenn.)

PLAIN AND PROSAIC TO THE
GROTESQUE NAMES

Alabama Squares
Arrow (N.C.)
Bachelor's Thumb (Ky.)
Bird's Eye
Bricks and Blocks
Buckens [sic] and Owls (R.I.)
Cat's Paw
Cat Track (Ky.)
Checkers
Cross Roads
Dimity
Dog Tracks (Mass.)
Dollars and Cents (Ky.)
Doors and Windows (Ky.)
Double Chain
Double Compass
Double Table
Flower Pot
Fool's Puzzle (Tenn.)
Forty-Nine Diamonds

Four Times (Va.)
Ginny Fowle (Ky. and Va.)
Green Veils
Hail Storm (N.C.)
Hen Scratch (Ky.)
Honeycomb (N.Y.)
Huckleberry
Ice Balls
Little Window Sash (Va.)
Locks and Dams (Ky.)
Log Cabin
Number Three (Va.)
Number Two (Va.)
Orange Peeling
Pea Fowl
Rattlesnake
Rattlesnake Trail (N.Y.)
Reed Canes, Panel Doors, and
   Window Sash (N.C.)
Rocky Mountain Cucumber
Shuckeroones (R.I.)
Sister Blankets
Sixteen Squares
Snail Trail
Snake Shed
Snow Storm
Snow Trail
Spectacles
Stripes and Squares
Sugar Loaf (Ky. and Tenn.)
Summer and Winter Wheel Draught
Wandering Winding Blades and
   Folding Windows (N.C. and Tenn.)
Wheels and Squares (Tenn.)
White House or American Beauty
Wild Mountain Cucumber (R.I.)
Winding Leaves and Folding Win-
   dows (N.C. and Tenn.)
Windows (Tenn.)
Windows and Doors (Ky.)
Window Sash (N.C.)
Window Sashes

VARIOUS BEAUTIES

Alabama Beauty
Baltimore Beauty
Beauty of New York
Boston Beauty
California Beauty
Captured Beauty
Everybody's Beauty
Four-Square Beauty
Kaintuck Beauty (Ky.)
Lasting Beauty (Va.)
Missouri Beauty (N.C.)
North Carolina Beauty
Parson's Beauty

Petersburg Beauty (Pa.)
Richmond Beauty
Rocky Mountain Beauty
Royal Beauty
Stolen Beauty
Troy's Beauty
Virginia Beauty

FANCIES, FAVORITES, DELIGHTS

Bachelor's Delight
Bachelor's Fancy (R.I.)
Diaman's Fancy
Dutchman's Fancy
Frenchman's Fancy
Gentleman's Fancy
Isaac's Favorite (N.C. and Tenn.)
King's Delight
Ladies' Delight
Lady's Fancy
Little Girl's Fancy
Maiden's Fancy
Mother's Favorite (Tenn.)
Queen's Delight
Rich Man's Fancy (N.C.)
Sally's Fancy
Solomon's Delight
Wheeler's Delight
Young Man's Fancy

CELESTIAL

Blazing Star
Little Blazing Star
Lone Star of Texas
Morning Star
Sea Star (N.C.)
Seven Stars (N.C.)
Star of the East (N.C.)
Sunrise (Ky.)
The Rising Sun
The Star of Venus
Virginia Star

WAVES

Floating Wave
Flourishing Wave
Ocean Wave

PERSON AND PLACE

Baltimore Street (Md.)
Brush Valley (Md.)
Cassie Rogan (Tenn.)
Cope (Tenn.)
Ellen Egger's Counterpane Draught
Eve Mast (Tenn.)
Hixson (Tenn.)
Isle of Patmos (Tenn.)
Mary (N.C.)
Miss Chester (N.C.)
Murphy's Legacy (Tenn.)
Old Duckett (N.C.)
Old Virginia
Owlsey Forks (Ky.)
South Country
St. Ann's Robe (Tenn.)

SENTIMENTAL

Friendship (Ky.)
Girls' Love
Lonely Heart (Ky.)
Lover's Chain (Pa.)
Lover's Knot (Pa.)
Soldier's Return (Tenn.)
True Lover's Knot (Va.)

WHEELS

Charity Wheel
Four Wheels
Iron Wheel (N.C.)
Methodist Wheel (N.C.)
Penford Chariot Wheels (Ky.)
Pilot Wheel (Ky.)
Running Wheel (Ky.)
Single Chariot Wheel (Ky.)
Single Wheel
Sixteen Chariot Wheels (Tenn.)
Sixteen Wheel Chariot (Tenn.)
Wheel and Squares
Wheel of Fancy
Wheel of Fortune
Wheel of Time (Minn.)

DIAMONDS

Broken Diamond (N.C.)
Cross and Diamond
Crown of Diamonds (N.C.)
Double Diamonds
Eight-Block Diamond
Half Diamond
Heart and Diamonds
Nine-Block Diamond
Square and Diamond
The King's Diamond

POLITICAL AND HISTORICAL

Battle of Richmond
Battle Union
Bonaparte's March
Bonaparte's Retreat
Braddock's Defeat (Ky.)
Confederate Flag
Cornwallis's Victory (Ky.)
Democrat Victory (N.C.)
Downfall of Paris (Ky. and N.C., 1815)
Indian Camp
Indian March
Indian War
Indian Warfare
Jackson's Army
Jay's Fancy
Jefferson's Fancy (N.J.)
Lady Washington's Delight
Lafayette's Fancy
Lee's Surrender
Maid of Orleans (Tenn.)
Martha Washington's Choice
Mexican Banner (Tenn.)
Missouri Trouble
Mount Vernon (Tenn.)
Perry's Victory

Polk and Dallas
Tennessee Trouble
Travis's Favorite
Washington's Diamond Ring (Va.)
Washington's Victory
Whig Rose

UNCLASSIFIED NAMES

Birds of the Air (N.Y.)
Bird's-Wye Coverlet
Blue and White Coverlet Number Three
Block Coverlet
Broken Snowballs
Capa's Number Five
Catch Me If You Can
Church Windows (Ky.)
Compass Diaper
Compass Work
Cross-a-Wise (Ireland, 1796)
Cuckoo's Nest (Ky.)
Double Bow Knot
Double Muscadine Hulls
Federal City (Ky.)
Federal Knot
Flag of Our Union
Flag Work
Flannery
Forty-Niners
Fox Trail (N.C.)
Freemason's Walk
Gardener's Note
Guess Me (N.C.)
Irish Chain
Job's Trouble (Tenn.)
Kentucky Snowflakes
Lady's Fancy Draught
Leopard Skin (N.C.)
Leopard Spots (Tenn.)
Little Checked
Mission Draught
New Jersey Dream
Old Glory
Prussian Diaper
Queen of England (Va.)
Queen's Household
Queen's Patch (Ky.)
Queen's Puzzle
Rings and Flowers of Virginia
Scarlet Balls
Single Chain
Spotted Leopard (Tenn.)
Squares of England
Summer and Winter
Tennessee Lace (Ky.)
Tennessee Trouble in North Carolina
The Bride's Table (Ky.)
The Globe (Ky.)
The Seashell
The Union Draught
Venus
Waffle Weave
Weaver's Choice
Weaver's Pleasure
Winding Girl (Ky.)
Work Complete
Young Lady's Perplexity (Ky.)

368 (left). A double Jacquard loom designed to speed up the operation of an earlier model that Jacquard had shown at an industrial exhibition in Paris in 1801.

369 (below). The first design for a Jacquard loom, showing the rows of cards with punched holes that control the operation of the harnesses.

THE JACQUARD COVERLET

A French weaver by the name of Joseph Jacquard invented a very sophisticated type of loom that first arrived in America about 1820 and was operated by hand with the flying shuttle. The Jacquard attachment could be added to the looms already in use for Double Weave coverlets, and thus the mechanization of weaving had begun. Jacquard's invention consisted of a series of cards with large and small punched holes that activated the harnesses of the loom (as many as forty by this time) and made the pattern. These cards resembled the music rolls used in a player piano.

The Jacquard loom made it possible for weavers to create large unseamed coverlets with handsome and complicated patterns. Elaborate borders became a distinguishing feature of this type, and the corners thus created gave the weaver a space in which to include his name, the name of the owner, and often the town, county, state, and date of weaving. Because of this we possess much precise information about the period and provenance of Jacquard coverlets.

The continued use of hand-spun and home-dyed wool for the weft permitted some feeling of handcraft in the earliest Jacquards, but they later became very mechanical. Hand weaving continued along with machine weaving in rural areas up to the time of the Civil War.

Undoubtedly there were many pattern books for the Jacquard loom, because many borders and motifs such as rosettes, urns, and eagles are used repeatedly. However, there is also a great deal of individuality to be seen in these coverlets, and the collecting of Jacquards is endlessly fascinating because of the variety of designs. Weavers became very proficient and could "punch" their cards so as to satisfy the design whims of their customers. The illustrations for this chapter ably demonstrate the immense variety of Jacquard patterns.

It was a favorite pastime of the weaver, after he had finished his work, to study the pattern and try to give it an appropriate name. It often happened, of course, that the same pattern could acquire several names in different communities. Many of these names for Jacquard coverlets accompany the illustrations. On pages 276–277 we list many of the professional weavers that have been identified by signed examples of their work. Dates have been included when they are known.

370 (above). Jacquard coverlet, Tile pattern with Christian and Heathen border (variation of the Boston Town border). 88″ × 46″. Inscribed "Adam Hoerr, Harmony, Butler Co., Pa., 1848." Blue on white. (Old Economy Village)

371 (above). Jacquard coverlet, Fancy Tile with Bird border. 86″ × 78″. Inscribed "J. Gamble, Weaver, 1834." (Denver Art Museum)

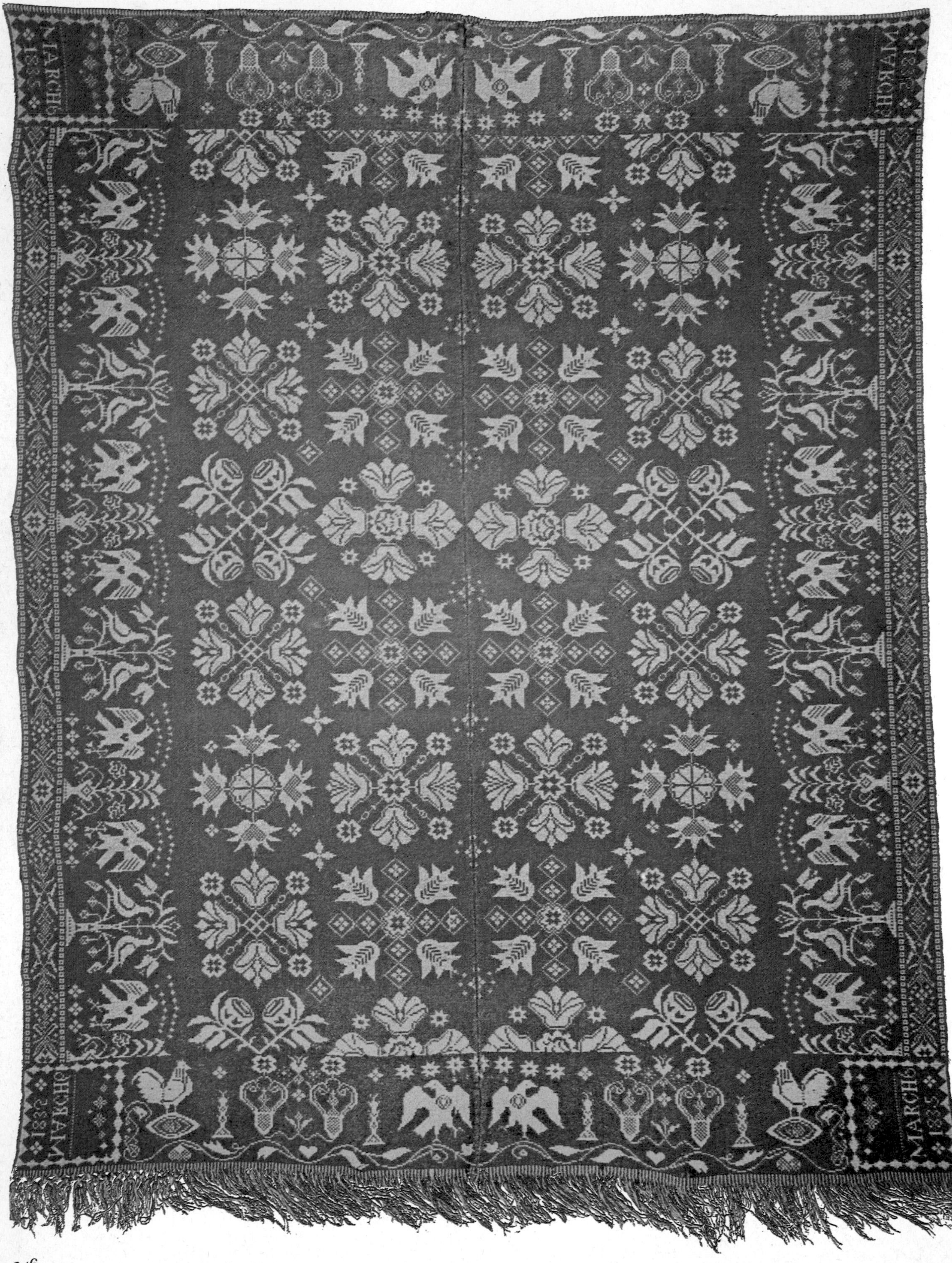
MARCH
1835

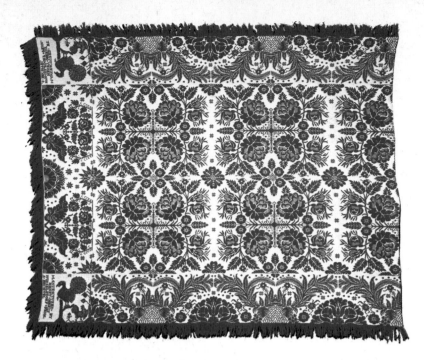

373 (above), 373a (below). Jacquard coverlet, Double Rose with fancy border, c. 1840. 104½″ × 89½″. Red wool on white. Inscribed "Manufactured by Henry Oberly, Womelsdorf, Penn., A. Bechtel." Mr. Bechtel was the customer. The detail below shows a turkey in a tree with a rooster below. (Privately owned)

372 (opposite). Jacquard coverlet, Double Lily with Eagle and Rooster border. 92½″ × 71″. Dated March 6, 1835. A lovely example of the Jacquard style, most unusual for the combination of two shades of blue. (Privately owned)

374 (above). Jacquard coverlet, Medallion with Fox and Hound border. 95½″ × 73″. Dark blue and white. Made by David D. Harlmz, weaver, October 14, 1833, for Jane Van Wagoner. (Privately owned)

375 (left), 375a (above). Double Weave Jacquard coverlet, True Boston Town pattern, c. 1840, showing Boston harbor with its sailing ships readying for the China trade. 91″ × 75″. The Oriental village above the New England town gives this coverlet the common title of "Christian and Heathen." The combination was often used in borders on later coverlets. The double grapevine and cable border is especially rich and elaborate. Blue wool on white cotton warp. (Henry Ford Museum)

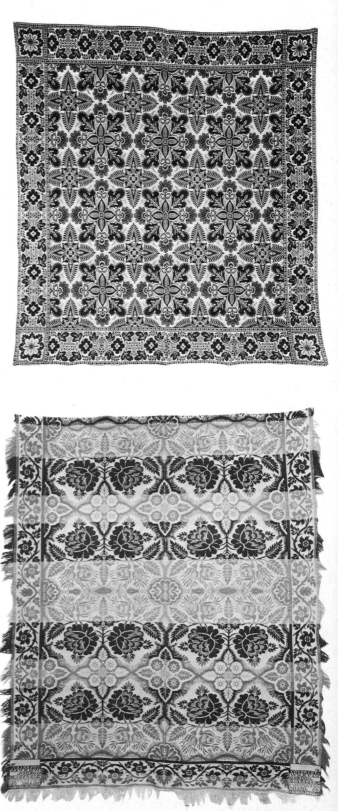

377 (above). Jacquard coverlet, Tile pattern with Bellflower border. 91″ × 78″. Woven by Samuel Graham in 1845. (Denver Art Museum)

379 (opposite, below right). Jacquard coverlet, Double Rose with Vine border. 91″ × 72″. Inscribed "Wm. H. Vangordon Coverlet Weaver, Covington, Miami Co., Ohio, 1852." (Denver Art Museum)

376 (opposite, above left), 376a, 376b, 376c (above). Jacquard coverlet, Sunburst and Double Lily with Harlequin border. 97¼″ × 83″. In the lower left corner it has the woven inscription "S. B. Musselman, Coverlet Weaver, Hiltaun, Bucks Co., No. 681." It is also inscribed in the lower right corner "This Coverlet Belongs to David Bonner 1847." Note how the inmost border has been formed out of the word "Pennsylvania." (Privately owned)

380 (above). Double Weave Jacquard coverlet, Medallion with Eagle and Tree border. 85″ × 80″. Inscribed "Mary Price; J. M. Davidson, Fancy Weaver, Lodi, 1836." Blue and white. (Faye and Don Walters)

381 (below). Jacquard coverlet, Geometric Tile with Eagle and Liberty border, c. 1868. 94″ × 74″. Blue and white. (Privately owned)

382 (center). Jacquard coverlet samples. Top: Rose Medallion with Wreath, Church and Eagle border. 34½″ × 33″. Bottom: Sunburst and Lily with Bird border. 33″ × 33″. Inscribed "C. K. Hinkel, Shippensburg, Cumberland County, Pa., 1841." Because of their small size, it is possible that these coverlets were intended for a child's use, but the large scale of the designs makes their function as weaver's samples much more probable. (Privately owned)

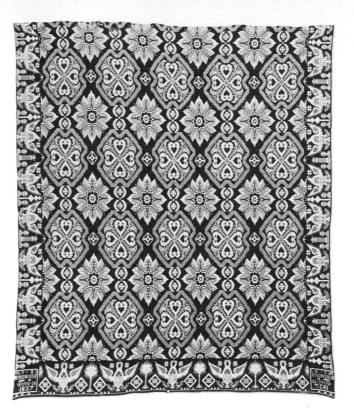

383 (above). Double Weave Jacquard coverlet, Tile with Eagle border. 87½″ × 76″. Woven by P. M. Morehouse in 1837. Indigo and white. (Faye and Don Walters)

384 (below). Double Weave Jacquard coverlet, Medallions with Eagle and Independence Hall border, 1876 (?). 92″ × 71″. Woven for Betsey Hayt and inscribed, "Agriculture and Manufactures Are the Foundation of Our Independence, July 4, 1826, General Lafayette." Indigo and white. (Henry Ford Museum)

385 (opposite, below), 385a (opposite, above). Jacquard coverlet, Medallion with Monkey and Tree border. 90″ × 79½″. Indigo and white. Made for J. P. Thomson in Jefferson County, New York, 1836. (Allan L. Daniel)

386 (center). Jacquard coverlet, Medallion with Lion and Tree border. 79″ × 69″. Woven in Zoar, Ohio, 1850. Blue on white. A particularly bold and handsome creation. (Henry Ford Museum)

387 (above). Double Weave Jacquard coverlet, Medallion with Rose Tree and Picket Fence border. Blue and white. Made for Mary Salisbury in Jefferson County, New York, 1842. (The New-York Historical Society)

389 (above). Jacquard coverlet, Fancy, c. 1850.
90″ × 78″. A very elaborate production including
vases of flowers, birds feeding their young, and a
Christian and Heathen border. (Privately owned)

388 (above), 388a (right). Jacquard coverlet, Sunburst
Tile center with Grapevine side border and Double Bird
and Roses on foot border. 90″ × 68¾″. Blue-green and
cream. Inscribed "John Klinhinz, Ohio, 1848." (Privately
owned)

390 (opposite). Detail of Double Weave Jacquard coverlet,
Turkey and Peacock, c. 1825. Simple border of Thistle
Leaf and Snow Drops. 91½″ × 73″. Red, white, and blue
on linen warp. (Henry Ford Museum)

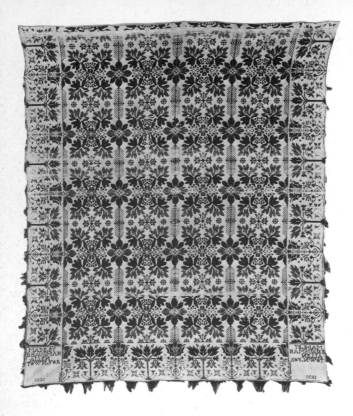

391 (left). Jacquard coverlet, Medallion, Double Oak Leaf with Tulip border. 96″ × 82″. Woven by B. Hausman of Allentown, Pennsylvania, 1838. Red, blue, and natural. (Privately owned)

393 (right). Jacquard coverlet, Sunburst Medallion with Potted Rose and Bird border, c. 1850. 90″ × 76″. Red, blue, and white. (Privately owned)

392 (left). Jacquard coverlet, Tile pattern with no border. 84″ × 74″. Red, blue, and white. (Privately owned)

394 (opposite). Jacquard coverlet, Medallion and Stripe, no border, c. 1850. 76″ × 90″. Single weave, navy and white. (Privately owned)

402 (left), 402a (below). Single Weave Jacquard coverlet, Tile pattern with Bellflower border on sides and a village and coastal schooners on foot border. 86″ × 71¼″. Blue and white. Inscribed "Year 1839." The date of 1839 makes it possible for this piece to have been made in Pennsylvania, Maryland, or Virginia. (Privately owned)

259

396 (right). Jacquard coverlet, Snowflake with Floral border. 88″ × 84″. Inscribed "J. Klein, Hamilton Co., Indiana, 1868." (Privately owned)

398 (opposite, above). Jacquard coverlet, Double Rose with Grapes and Leaves border. 96″ × 82″. Wm. Lowmiller, weaver, 1845. (Privately owned)

399 (opposite, below). Detail of a Jacquard coverlet, Tile pattern with Bird border. 85″ × 76″. Inscribed "Indiana, By D. I. G., 1837." Blue wool on white linen. (San Antonio Museum Association)

395 (above). Jacquard coverlet, Double Rose with Bird border. 94″ × 80″. Inscribed "Gabriel Rauser, Delaware County, Ohio, 1843." Blue and red on dark natural. (Privately owned)

397 (right). Jacquard coverlet, Fancy Tile with Double Vine border. 92″ × 86″. Inscribed "Manufactured by D. Pursell, Portsmouth, Ohio." (Privately owned)

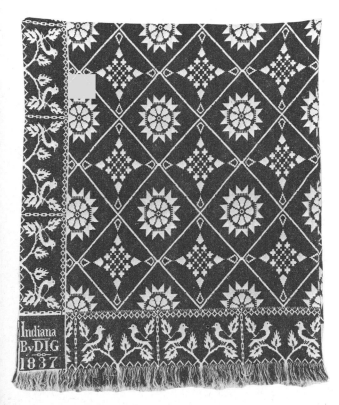

400 (above). Jacquard coverlet, Double Rose with a triple Bird border. 98″ × 82″. Inscribed "E. Fordenbach, 1843." (Privately owned)

401 (below). Jacquard coverlet, Sunburst and Double Lily with Partridge border. 94″ × 76″. Inscribed "Made by J. Denholm, 1839." (Privately owned)

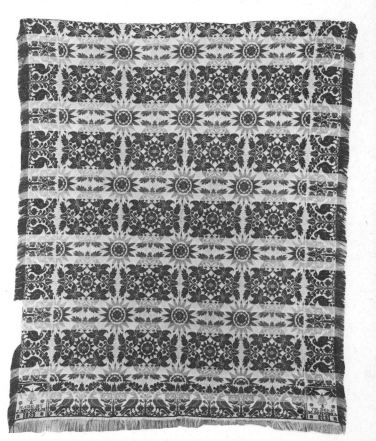

402 (left), 402a (below). Single Weave Jacquard coverlet, Tile pattern with Bellflower border on sides and a village and coastal schooners on foot border. 86″ × 71¼″. Blue and white. Inscribed "Year 1839." The date of 1839 makes it possible for this piece to have been made in Pennsylvania, Maryland, or Virginia. (Privately owned)

403 (right). Details of a Double Weave Jacquard coverlet, Exotic Birds feeding their young, with Christian and Heathen border, dated 1844. 92″ × 70″. Indigo and white. In the photograph we see both sides of this spread, clearly showing that one side is exactly the reverse of the other (Henry Ford Museum)

404 (above), 404a (opposite, below). Double Weave Jacquard coverlet, Snowflake Medallion with the Hemfield Railroad border, 1850. 89″ × 79″. This is a rare coverlet since only five examples are known to exist. It commemorates the opening of the railroad. However, the location of the railroad has never been identified. The profile in the corners is of the first president, T. McKennan. The weavers who are known to have made these coverlets are: Daniel Campbell, William Harper, Martin Burns, George Coulter, and Harvey Cook. (Privately owned)

405 (below), 405a (left). Detail of a Jacquard coverlet, Rose Medallion with Tulip border on sides, and Double Train at the foot border. Made by Peter Grimm in 1857, Loudonville, Ohio. (Henry Ford Museum)

406 (above), 406a (center). Single Weave Jacquard coverlet, 1848. Tile pattern with True Boston Town border. 98″ × 77″. Blue and white. (Privately owned)

407 (below). Jacquard coverlet, Oak Leaf with Oak Tree border. 94″ × 83″. J. Lantz, weaver, 1837. Red, blue, and green on white. (Privately owned)

408 (above). Double Weave Jacquard coverlet, Tile pattern with Christian and Heathen border. 94″ × 75″. Adam Hoerr, weaver, 1856. Rust and dark blue on white. (Old Economy Village)

409 (below). Single Weave Jacquard coverlet, Centennial pattern: Memorial Hall with Floral border, 1876. 89¾″ × 80″. Red wool on white warp. (Philadelphia Museum of Art)

410 (below), 410a (bottom). Jacquard coverlet, Medallion with Running Stag border on sides and E Pluribus Unum on foot border. 88″ × 73″. Inscribed "Woven at the Ithaca Carpet Factory by Archibald Davidson, 1838." (Privately owned)

411 (above). Jacquard coverlet, exactly same pattern as example at left, but in reverse color scheme. 90″ × 80″. Woven by Archibald Davidson in 1840. (Henry Ford Museum)

412 (below). Jacquard coverlet, Shield-bodied American Eagle with Floral border,
c. 1840. 80″ × 46″. Blue, brown, red, light green, and tan on white warp.
(The New-York Historical Society)

413 (opposite). Double Weave Jacquard coverlet, Medallion pattern with Masonic symbols. The border is completely composed of Masonic symbols. 94″ × 75½″. The weaver is unknown, and the coverlet is not dated. Blue and white. (Privately owned)

414 (right), 414a (above). Jacquard coverlet, Tile pattern with Potted Flower border. 94¼″ × 92½″. Red, black, and green on white warp. One of a pair, dated 1854. The use of the alphabet in every other black block is unusual, and it is also unusual that it only goes through L. (Privately owned)

415 (below), 415a (above), 415b (above, right). Jacquard coverlet, Large Medallion with Eagle border. 89″ × 75″. In each of the four corners George Washington in full military regalia is astride his horse. Inscribed "United We Stand, Divided We Fall" and "Under This We Prosper." Made by J. Cunningham, North Hartford, Oneida County, New York, 1845. Blue and white. (Privately owned)

416 (center). Double Weave Jacquard coverlet, Medallion with Capitol in laurel wreath, with Double Rose border. 86″ × 78″. Dated 1846. Blue and rust on white. (The New-York Historical Society)

417 (right). Double Weave Jacquard coverlet, Tile and Double Rose with House border (variation of Boston Town). 84″ × 68″. Woven for Jane E. Hallack, 1840. Blue and white. (Privately owned)

418 (below, right). Double Weave Jacquard coverlet, The Great Seal of the United States enclosed in a grapevine wreath, 1831. Star field with Thistle leaf border. (Old Economy Village)

419 (below). Jacquard coverlet, large central Medallion with the head of Miss Liberty, flanked by laurel branches, repeated four times. Wide fancy scroll border with shield-bodied eagles in the corners. 96″ × 82″. Woven in 1849 in Palmyra, New York, by J. Van Ness. (Privately owned)

420 (above). Jacquard coverlet, large oval Medallion with Wreath and large leaves, scrolls, and urns in field. 88½″ × 78¼″. Gold on red ground. (Privately owned).

421 (right). Jacquard coverlet, Floral Medallion and four large Roses in field, border of Grapes and Leaves in separate units, and four Snowflake corners. 98½″ × 76½″. Inscribed "Mary Emigh, AD 1848, Washington." Blue and white. (Privately owned)

422 (opposite, above). Jacquard coverlet, elaborate Tile pattern with small Grape border. An unusual detail is the tiny drums included in the borders of the blue-and-white rectangles. Dated 1849. 86″ × 74¼″. Resembles an ingrain-carpet design. (Privately owned)

423 (opposite, below). Jacquard coverlet, Medallion with Wreath surrounded by eight spread eagles, stags, and birds. Narrow classic border. 92″ × 86″. Dated 1856. (Gary R. Davenport)

PROFESSIONAL WEAVERS

Adam, ——. (Greencastle, Franklin Co., Pa.), 1821
Adolf, Charles (Henry Co., Ind.), 1857
Adolf, George (Henry Co., Ind.), 1857
Adolf, Henry (Hamilton Co., Ind.), 1851
Akin, Phebe (N. Y.), 1834
Alexander, F. M., 1848
Alexander, Robert (Canfield, O.), 1850
Allabach, Philip (Mich.)
Allen, A. (O.), 1840
Ardner, Jacob and Michael (Mount Vernon, Knox Co., O.), 1858
Artman, Abraham (Dansville, N. Y.), 1830
Ball, H. H. (Orange Co., N. Y.), 1830
Balantyne, ——. (Ind.), 1845, 1849
Baird, James (Switzerland Co., Ind.), 1830
Bartlet, Jerusha, 1855
Beil, B., 1846
Bichel, W. (Newark, O.), 1843
Biesecker, J., Jr., 1852
Bissett, ——. (Franklin, Ind.)
Bivenouer, M., 1842
Bordner, Daniel (Millersburg, Berks Co., Pa.), 1839
Brand, D., 1838
Brehm, Henry (Womelsdorf, Berks Co., Pa.), 1836
Breneman, Martin B. (York Co., Pa.), 1861
Brick, Zena, 1833
Broson, J. & R. (Utica, N. Y.), 1817
Brosey, J., 1838
Brosey, W., 1847
Brown, John (N. Y.), 1843
Brubaker, A., 1847
Buechel, W. (Logan Co., O.), 1847
Burkerd, E. (La Porte, Ind.), 1845
Burns, Martin (W. Va.), 1851
Butterfield, J. (New Hartford, Oneida Co., N. Y.)
Calister, James C. (Jefferson Co., N. Y.), 1853
Campbell, Daniel (Bridgeport, W. Va.), 1839
Chappelear, Mary, 1856
Conger, J. (N. Y.), 1839
Conner, C. S., 1839
Cook, Harvey (W. Va.), 1851
Cole, J. C. (Vernon Township, Crawford Co., O.), 1861
Collings, S., 1834
Colman, Peter (O.), 1853
Cosley, D. (Xenia, Green Co., O.), 1850
Cosley, G. (Xenia, O.), 1851
Coulter, George (W. Va.), 1851
Cowam, Donald (Switzerland Co., Ind.), 1820
Covey, Harriet (N. Y.), 1840
Craig, J. (Floyd Co., Ind.)
Graig, William, Jr. (Greensburg, Decatur Co., Ind.), 1850
Graig, William, Sr. (Greensburg, Decatur Co., Ind.), 1838
Cranston, Thomas (Switzerland Co., Ind.), 1855
Crozier, John (Cadiz, O.), 1830, 1840
Cunningham, J. (New Hartford, Oneida Co., N. Y.), 1837
Davidson, Archibald (Ithaca, N. Y.), 1832, 1840
Davidson, J. M. (Lodi, O.), 1837
Deavler, Joseph, 1841
Dengler, John (Newry, Blair Co.,?), 1850
Denholm, J., 1839
Deyarmon, Abraham (Lexington, Ky.), 1825

Enders, Henry (Sidney, Shelby Co., O.), 1876
Ettinger, Emanuel (Aaronsburg, Center Co., Pa.), 1834, 1841
Fairbrothers, William (Henry Co., Ind.)
Fehr, C. (Emaus, ?) 1839
Forden, E. (Bach, ?), 1813
France, Joseph (R. I.), 1814
Frances, ——. (Ind.)
Franz, Michael (Miami Co., O.), 1839
Frazie, J. (Casey, Ill.), 1861
French, B. (Clinton, ?), 1840
Gambel, J., 1834
Gamble, Sam (Glasgow, Ky.)
Garber, C. (Ruffs Creek, Green Co., Pa.), 1840
Garrett, Thomas (Hagerstown, Md.), 1804
Gebhart, J. (Pa.)
Gernand, J. B. (Md.)
Gernand, W. H. (Westminster, Carroll Co., Md.), 1873
Getty, A. (Lockport, N. Y.)
Getty, J. A. (Ind.)
Gilchrist, Hugh (Franklin Co., Ind.), 1869
Gilmore, Gabriel (Union Co., Ind.), 1826
Gilmore, Joseph, Thomas, and William (Union Co., Ind.), 1826
Gilmore, William (moved to Oskloosa, Ia.), 1858
Goodman, John S. (Black Creek, Luzern Co., Pa.), 1830
Goodwin, Harmon (Me.)
Graham, John (Morris Township, Nox Co., O.), 1853
Graham, Samuel (Newcastle, Ind.), 1841
Graves, David Isaac (Morgan Co., Ind.), 1836, 1839
Grimm, Peter (Loundonville, Ashlan Co., O.), 1851, 1867
Hadsell, Ira (Palmyra, N. Y.), 1849, 1866
Hall, ——. 1869
Hamilton, John (Lanark, Ill.), 1850
Harch, J.
Harlme, David D.
Harper, William (Bridgeport, W. Va.), 1839
Hart, ——. 1851
Hartman, John (Lafayette, O.), 1845, 1851
Hartman, Peter (La Fayette, Wooster, O.), 1843, 1845
Hausman, Allan B. (Groveland, N. Y.), 1839
Hausman, Benjamin (Allentown, Pa.), 1858
Hausman, Ephraim (Trexlertown, Berks Co., Pa.), 1850
Hausman, Jacob, Jr. (Lobachsvill, Friedensburg, Rockland, Berks Co., Pa.), 1846
Hausman, Jacob, Sr. (Lobachsvill, Berks Co., Pa.), 1838
Hausman, Solomon (Trexlertown, Berks Co., Pa.), 1848
Hausman, Tilgham (Lobachsvill, Berks Co., Pa.)
Hecht, Abslam (Md.), 1849
Heilbronn, G. (Lancaster, Basil, O.), 1839, 1850
Heilbronn, J. J. (Basil, O.), 1839
Hesse L. (Somerset, O.), 1847
Hicks, William (Madison Co., Ind.), 1850
Hinkel, C. K. (Shippensburg, Cumberland Co., Pa.), 1841
Hogeland, J. S. and son (Lafayette, Ind.), 1856
Hohulin, Gottlich, 1861
Hoke, M. (Dover, York Co., Pa.), 1842, 1847
Hopeman, ——. (N. Y.)
Housman, ——. 1839, 1845
Huber, John and Damus (Dearborn Co., Ind.), 1840, 1850
Hudders, J. S. (Bucks Co., Pa.), 1849
Hull, Mathias
Humphreys, S. (Bethany, Genesee Co., N.Y.), 1835

Impson, J. (Cortland Co., N. Y.), 1845
Ingham, J. & D., 1847
Irwin, L. (Pulaski, N. Y.), 1859
Jackson, John Hamilton (Pa.), 1840
Kappel, Gottfried & Co. (Zoar, O.), 1845, 1871
Kaufman, John, 1843
Kean, C. L. (Scott Co., Ky.), 1850, 1860
Kean, F. A. (Terre Haute, Vigo Co., Ind.), 1838, 1851
Kerns, William (Parke Co., Ind.)
Kepner, Isaac (Pottstown, Montgomery Co., Pa.), 1843
Klar, Francis Joseph, 1843
Klehl, J. (Hamilton Co., Ind.), 1868
Klein, John (Noblesville, Hamilton Co., Ind.), 1861
Klinger, Absalom (Millersburg, Berks Co., Pa.), 1854
Landes, John, 1805
Lantz, J. (East Hemfield Township, Pa.), 1837
Lashel, ——. (O.), 1850
La Tourette, John (Fountain Co., Ind.), 1826
La Tourette, Henry and Sarah (Fountain Co., Ind.)
Le Bar, Pamela (North Hampton Co., Pa.), 1843
Leitz, ——. (Milwaukee, Wisc.), 1850
Lichy, B. (Bristol, O.), 1854
Lorentz, Peter (Wayne Co., Ind.), 1838
Lowmiller, William (Muncey, Boroly Co., Ind.)
Lutz, J. (Hempfield Township, ?), 1850, 1856
MacKeon, Abraham B., 1841
March, J. H. (Salona, Clinton Co., Pa.), 1840, 1841
Marr, John (Milton, Ind.), 1843
Marsh, J., 1840
Marsteller, Thomas (Lower Saucon, ?), 1845
McKinney, James (Brookville, Ind.), 1813
Mealy, ——. (Milwaukee, Wisc.), 1850
Meily, Charles S. (Mansfield, Wayne Co., O.), 1837
Mellinger, John & Sons (Seneca Co., Pa.), 1836
Mench, E., 1840
Mesick, C., 1836
Metz, L. (Montgomery Co., Pa.), 1841
Metzger, F. (Pa.)
Miller, Gabriel (Pa.), 1820
Miller, Levi M. S. (Hancock Co., Jackson Township, O.), 1860
Miller, Robert (Salem, Ind.), 1857, 1858
Miller, Tobias (LaGrange Co., Ind.), 1867
Milroy, ——. (Miffin Co., Pa.), 1851
Morrey, ——. (O.)
Muir, John (Greencastle, Ind.), 1843
Muir, Robert, Thomas, and William (Germantown, Wayne Co., Ind.)
Muir, William (Germantown, 1836; moved 1842 to Indianpolis, Ind.), 1850
Mundwiler, Samuel (Hopewell Township, O.), 1848
Musselman, S. B. (Hiltaun, Bucks Co., Pa.), 1847
Myer, P., 1841
Myers, D. L. (Bethel Township, ?), 1849
Nash, Matilda (Switzerland Co., Ind.) (from Ireland), 1838
Ney, William (Myerston, Pa.)
Nicklas, G. (Chambersburg, Franklin Co., Pa.), 1840, 1843
Noll, William and John, 1872
Nurre, Joseph (Dearborn Co., Ind.), 1839
Oberly, Henry (Womelsdorf, Pa.), 1850
Oppel, C. & Co. (Zoar, O.), 1850
Orms, ——. (Malago, O.)
Ott, C. (Franklin Township, Richland Co., O.), 1844
Overholt, Henry O., 1842
Packer, J. (Brownsville, Fisher Co., Pa.), 1839
Pearsen, J. (Chippeway, ?)
Petrie, ——. (near Albany, N. Y.)
Petry, H. (Canton, O.), 1842
Pierce, Merrily, 1834
Pompey, L. W., 1831
Pursell, D. (Portsmouth, O.), 1840, 1850
Randell, Martha (Chardo, O.), 1848
Rausher, Gabriel (O. and Pa.), 1840, 1853
Rassweiler, Ph. (Orwigsburg, Pa.), 1844
Reed, V. R. (Benton, N. Y.), 1883
Rich, John (Clinton Co., Pa.), 1854

Richardson, ——. 1835
Rose, William Henry Harrison (R. I.), 1860
Rossvilles, ——. (N. Y.), 1851
Rouser, Gabriel (Delaware Co., O.), 1843
Salisbury, Henry, 1849
Salisbury, Mary (Jefferson, N. Y.), 1842
Sayels, J. M. (Clinton Co., Ill.), 1851
Schnee, Joseph (Freeburg, Pa.), 1836
Schnee, William (Freeburg, Pa.), 1838
Schrontz, ——. (Dearborn Co., Ind.)
Seibert, John (Lowhill Township, Lehigh Co., Pa.), 1846
Sheafer, Franklin D., 1849
Sheaffer, Isaac (New Berlin, ?), 1842, 1845
Sherman, Jacob (Attica, Seneca Co., O.), 1838
Sherman, John (Mt. Morris, Genesee Co., N. Y.), 1838
Schum, Philip (Lancaster, Pa.), 1869
Shotwell, ——. (Shotwell's Landing [Rahway], N. J.), 1845
Simpson, George (Switzerland Co., Ind.), 1840
Singer, J. (Osnaburg Township, Stark Co., O.), 1846
Snider, Samuel, 1843
Snyder, Jacob (Strake Co., O.), 1849
Snyder, John (Milton, Ind.), 1843
Snyder, Mary (Tappan, N. Y.), 1837
Speck, Johan (Pa.), 1825
Stager, H. F. (Mount Joy, Lancaster Co., Pa.)
Staples, Waity (Ill.), 1810
Staudt, Simon (Miami Co., O.), 1845
Steier, W. (Hanover Township, Montgomery Co., Pa.), 1848
Steinhiler, M. (Ross Co., O.), 1843
Stephenson, D. (Fairfield, Ia.), 1849
Sternberg, William (N. Y.), 1838
Stich, G. (Newark, O.), 1839
Stick, G. (O.), 1848
Stiff, Jay (Pa.), 1843
Stracke, Barnhardt (Hocking Co., O.), 1856
Striebig, John (Wayne Co., Ind.), 1834, 1840
Stringer, Samuel (Carthage, Rush Co., Ind.), 1848
Strobel, Lorenz (O.), 1846
Thompson, Ritchie (Brownsville, Ind.), 1834
Trappe, Samuel J., 1856
Tyler, Harry (Butterville, Jefferson Co., N. Y.), 1834, 1840
Umbarger, Michael (Dauphin Co., Pa.), 1851
Van Doren A. W. (Avon, Oakland Co., Mich.), 1845
Van Gordon, Wm. H. (Covington, Miami Co., O.), 1852
Van Ness, J. (Palmyra, N. Y.), 1848, 1850
Van Nortwic, C. (Ashbury, N. J.), 1840
Van Sickle, Sarah "LaTourrette" (Married name, married twice), 1850
Vanvleck, Jay A. (O.)
Varick, ——. 1835
Verplank, Samuel (Fishkill, Dutchess Co., N. Y.), 1843
Vogel, ——. (Cawfordsville, Ind.), 1846
Warick, J., 1849
Weaver, John W. (Rowsburg, Ashland Co., O.), 1852
Welty, John B. (Washington Co., Boonsboro, Md.), 1848
Whitmer, J. (Manor Township, Lancaster Co., Pa.), 1838
Wiand, C. (Allentown, Pa.), 1854
Wiand, David (Zieglersville, Pa.), 1837
Wilkison, Emily (Bethany, Genesee Co., N. Y.), 1836
William, Abram (Avon Township, Mich.), 1838, 1864
Wilson, Henry (Hendricks Co., New Winchester, Ind.), 1850, 1852
Wingert, George S. (Landisburg, Perry Co., Pa.), 1838
Wingert, H. (Landisburg, Perry Co., Pa.), 1846
Wirick, J. (Midway, Clark Co., O.), 1849
Wissler, John [afterward: Whisler] (Milton, Ind.), 1826, 1843
Witmer, J. (Lancaster Co., Pa.), 1841
Witt, ——. (N. Y.), 1847
Wohe, W. (Pittsford, Hillsdale Co., Mich.), 1860
Wolf, Adam (O.), 1849
Wolfe, W. (Pittsford, Hillsdale Co., Mich.), 1860
Yardy, C. (Lampeter Square, ?), 1833
Yearous, F. (Ashland Co., O.), 1853
Young, Matthew (Canton, Ind.)

THE CANDLEWICK SPREAD

"Candlewicking" is a type of bedcovering often passed over in a discussion of weaving, and it is found infrequently, usually undated and unsigned. There are actually two types of work called candlewicking, only because both use a coarse, soft, white cording or "roving" resembling the wicks used by candlemakers. The roving was an inexpensive type of twisted cotton.

The woven type of candlewick spread is probably exclusively American and was produced about 1820 and for a short time thereafter. Embroidered candlewicking lasted much longer, and machine-made derivatives of this type can still be seen on any tourist route through the South. There are a few examples known where the roving is used both as a shuttle thread and as embroidery.

The woven spread that belonged to Mrs. George Mason of Gunston Hall in Virginia is one of the best examples that survives. It is ninety-two inches wide and lacks a center seam, so it would have required a large loom and two boys to throw the shuttles to assist the weaver. It was woven with a fine cotton warp, and a weft shuttle wound with roving. The pattern was made by the weaver picking up with a "reed" certain loops of the roving from the flat weaving. The reed held the loops while he treadled the warp encircling the wicking, thus holding the loops firmly. Anyone who has seen modern "pile" carpet being woven will recognize that this is basically the principle of tufting. Sometimes a weaver used two reeds of different diameters and by using these he was able to create a deep-pile pattern and a low-pile pattern on the same spread. The effect was like a halftone instead of a simpler two-tone spread.

Another example of a woven candlewick spread deserves special mention because it carries the inscription, "Col. Henry Rutgers 1822," woven in the bottom border. Part of the center design includes the "Rutgers Factory." A coverlet mill was built in Paterson, New Jersey, in 1801, and by 1814 fourteen cotton mills were listed in the village containing two hundred forty-nine power looms, seventy-nine hand looms, and one counterpane weaver. The pattern of the Rutgers coverlet closely resembles the type done on the Jacquard looms, with an eagle in the center surrounded by stars. The rest of the pattern comprises diagonals going to the four corners of the spread with squared off "tulips" and a zigzag diamond border of swags and tassels.

The type of candlewick spread that is embroidered with the roving instead of wool or silk is probably a descendant of seventeenth-century English needlework. These spreads are usually made of a linen or cotton twill, with the design made of French knots in a lighter-weight roving, and the heavier cord "laid and couched" as in crewel. There are several examples of late eighteenth- and early nineteenth-century embroideries with "wicking" worked through light cotton dimity or homespun with each stitch raised by passing the loop over a twig, thus making a series of running stitches that are sometimes cut. It is a process somewhat similar to making chenille today. If a housewife today desires to make a tufted spread, she buys cotton that has not been shrunk, embroiders it very coarsely, and washes it to shrink and tighten the stitches. By shearing the design to create tufts, the modern chenille spread is created.

Embroidered candlewick spreads became more numerous about 1825, and of these we illustrate an outstanding example (figure 424) from the Titus Geesey collection, now in the Philadelphia Museum of Art. It is made of horizontally ribbed cotton and is completely embroidered in French knots of two sizes. The center medallion features an eagle surrounded by seventeen stars. The other motifs of baskets and urns, grapes and flowers remind us of early crewel and quilting patterns.

424 (opposite). Embroidered candlewick spread with two sizes of French knots on horizontally ribbed cotton. Pennsylvania German, c. 1810. 105″ × 78″. (Titus C. Geesey Collection, Philadelphia Museum of Art)

425 (right). Detail of a candlewick spread. Dated and inscribed in candlewicking, "1820, Katurah Reeve Her Work, When This You See Remember Me When I Am in Eternity." (Winterthur Museum)

426 (opposite, above). Embroidered candlewick spread in two weights of plain cotton 76" × 64". The roving appears to have been applied in several strands, stitched in place, and then cut to make a continuous raised line. Some units of the design are done in finer roving and are uncut. Inscribed "M. A. Todd, 1837." (Ginsburg & Levy, Inc.)

427 (opposite, below). Woven candlewick spread, c. 1810. The decoration is formed by loops of roving held in place by the warp thread. 119" × 80". The design of this white coverlet comprises the usual series of borders in geometrical designs, flowers, tassels, and chains. (Philadelphia Museum of Art)

428 (above). Woven candlewick spread. The elaborate design is made even more so by the addition of straight and scalloped fringes on the sides and bottom. The following inscription has been woven into the top border of this major example of the candlewick style: "This Was Begun By Mary M. Rounds, Buckfield, March 1, 1833, Who Died Aug. 21, 1833, Age 20, Finished By Fanny Andrews, Hartford, Oct. 15, 1835." (Ginsburg & Levy, Inc.)

429 (opposite), 429a (below). Embroidered candlewick spread, with several sizes of roving used, some sheared, c. 1825. 79¾" × 65¾". A Tree-of-Life design with two large birds, embroidered and sheared. The tree is in outline stitch, French knots, and satin stitch. The shocks of wheat are in sheared satin-stitched outline. The two deer have sheared bodies; the trees are uncut satin-stitch with fruit or foliage of sheared puffs. (Privately owned)

430 (right). Embroidered candlewick spread, c. 1840. 108" × 100". One size of roving is used throughout the design, and it is "couched" or caught in place and held by a finer thread in a close stitch. The design bears a certain resemblance to the woven spread on page 281. (Ginsburg & Levy, Inc.)

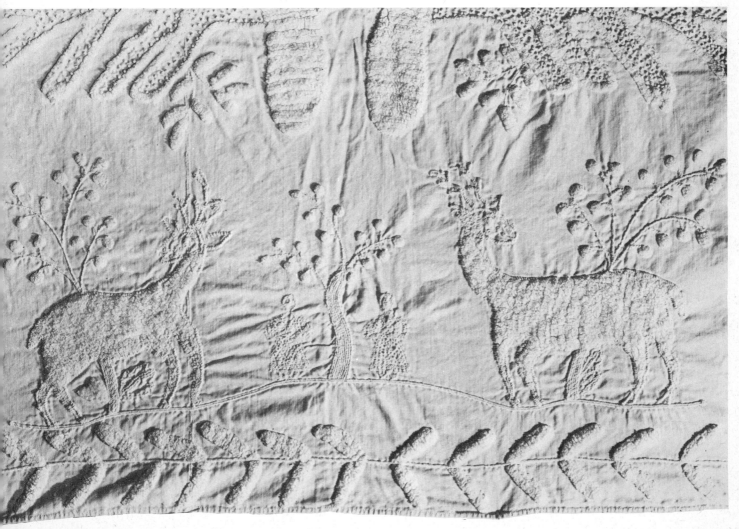

431 (above). Embroidered candlewick spread. 104" × 90½".
Fine roving was used for the French knots that make up
most of the design—the basket, stars, leaves, and swags. The
tufts are made of coarser roving and are sheared. Inscribed
"Sarah A. Quinby, Aged 21. 1843." (Privately owned)

432 (above). Embroidered candlewick spread, c. 1830. 101" × 91". A design that much resembles a woven candlewick. Architectural and geometric motifs completely made in French knots of two or more sizes, and some stem stitch. (Cincinnati Art Museum)

431a (center). This detail from the Quinby spread contains a splendid "vocabulary" of candlewick embroidery stitches that may be studied at close hand.

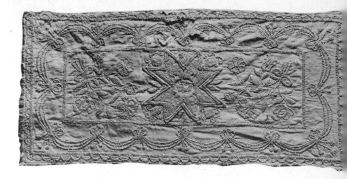

433 (below). Woven candlewick spread. 108¾″ × 103¾″. The design is built up with one row of roving to two regular threads of weft, the latter holding the loops of the design in place. Along the bottom a woven inscription reads: "To Solomon and Sarah Higgins from Their Friends of the Congregation of St. John's M. E. Church 1847." Also, all the names of the congregation have been woven into the spread by George F. Little, who signed the piece at the lower right. (Philadelphia Museum of Art)

434 (opposite, above), 435 (left). Embroidered candlewick pillow cover (42″ × 20″) and spread (100″ × 96″) made c. 1812 by Phoebe Cotheal, New York. Both pieces are chiefly made of French knots. (The New-York Historical Society)

436 (below). Embroidered candlewick spread, c. 1830. 114½″ × 85½″. A wonderfully elaborate and unusual design of the sun, crescent moons, swans, birds, flowers, grapes, and interlocking circles. (Privately owned)

437 (left). Detail of a woven candlewick spread, indigo roving with white warp and weft. 105″ × 97″. The designs are constructed in the same manner as the all-white spreads, but because of the strong color contrast, they are more emphatic. The overall pattern is geometric, consisting of a series of square borders centered with an octagonal motif. The coverlet is inscribed, "Emily Edson Jones No. 1." (Henry Ford Museum)

438 (below, left). Woven candlewick spread of the same design and colors as figures 437 and 439. The top of the spread carries this woven inscription: "L. N. Whitehouse no. 177 1839 H. W. Aged 72." These woven candlewicks combining two colors are great rarities. (Wadsworth Atheneum)

439 (below), 439a (middle, left), 439b (opposite). Woven candlewick spread, indigo and white, in the same pattern as figures 437 and 438. 97″ × 97″. The top carries the woven inscription: "Liberty N. Whitehouse no. 47 1833." What can we surmise from these last two examples? Perhaps Whitehouse was the weaver recording the number of spreads of this type he had woven by 1833 and 1839; or perhaps Whitehouse was the client (an innkeeper of some sort?) who liked his spreads numbered and dated, thus making the "H. W. Aged 72" of figure 438 the signature of the weaver. It would be interesting to know the true facts. (Privately owned)

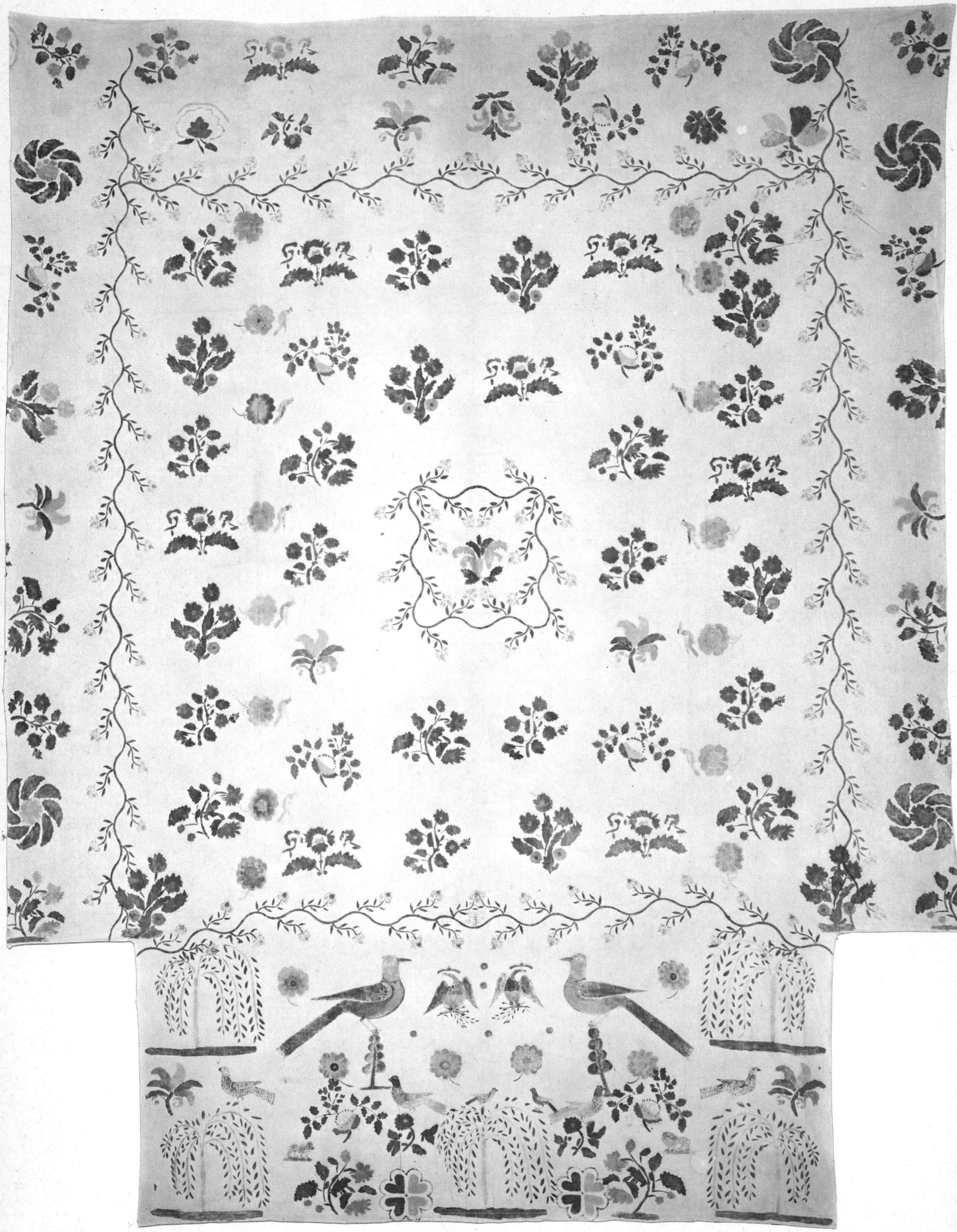

THE STENCIL SPREAD

The stencil spread is a lovely and fascinating product of the period, approximately from 1820 to 1840, that produced handsomely stenciled walls, floors, and furniture, chiefly in the eastern states. The stencil quilt seems to have been intended more to decorate a bed than used for warmth, for only a very few quilted examples are known. Possibly such spreads were intended to be used only during the summer, since they are unlined as well as unquilted. Examples of stencil quilts are very rare now, and it is a curious fact that most examples that do exist are almost new in appearance. The fashion for such coverlets seems to have been limited to rural areas.

The stenciling process was quite simple. The designs seen in our illustrations were traced on oiled paper and cut out with scissors or a sharp knife—one stencil for each color to be used. The spread of inexpensive cotton was placed flat on a slightly padded table and stretched so that it could not move. The overall plan for the placement of the individual stencils was marked on the cloth, and the actual work was ready to begin. Colors were prepared in two ways. A concentrated dye could be mixed with gum arabic so it would not run under the stencil and blur the sharp edges, but it was difficult to set the color and fading occurred almost immediately. The commoner method was to use ground pigment in oil from the hardware store and mix this with a formula called stencil mordant, which set the colors more permanently. The paint was tamped through the openings in the stencils onto the fabric, one color being done at a time, and with a drying period after each color was applied. The colors were in some cases allowed to become lighter around the edges of the design to suggest a third dimension to the pattern. The tampon was a ball of cotton firmly held in shape with a coarse cotton cover that soaked up the paint.

The American Museum in Bath, England, owns a fine example of a quilted stencil spread from Connecticut. The museums at Cooperstown, New York, Shelburne, Vermont, and the Henry Ford Museum in Dearborn, Michigan, have examples of stencil spreads all done on muslin or fine linen. Stenciled tablecloths and table scarves are found more often than bedspreads.

440 (opposite), 440a (left), 440b (above). Stencil spread, unquilted, c. 1825, New York (?). 100″ × 76½″. A particularly lovely example of the stencil style in coverlets, this piece features repeated motifs of flowers, birds, shield-bodied eagles, weeping willows, and two tiny lions. Note the minute birds perched on top of the blossoms on the right and left sides of the center section of the spread. (Privately owned)

441 (above). Stencil spread, quilted, c. 1835, New York (?). 89½″ × 77½″. A typical example of stenciling, with two rows of roses facing each other and a repeated border motif. The blossoms and buds are pale red-orange with blue-green stems and leaves. (Privately owned)

442 (center), 442a (opposite, below), 442b (above). Stencil spread, unquilted, c. 1830, New York or New England. 96½″ × 86″. A very ambitious and colorful example of stenciling constructed of many motifs that have been combined into a successful whole. The design was probably started in the center and worked outward toward the edges. (Privately owned)

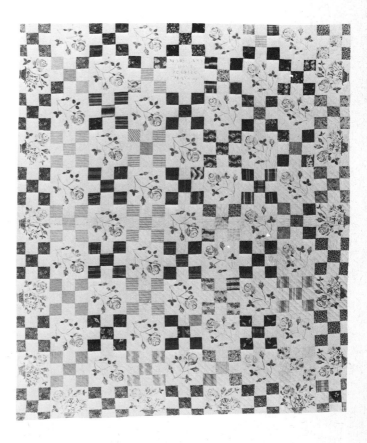

443 (right). Patchwork quilt with stenciled blocks, Pennsylvania. Inscribed "Mary Ann Hoyt, Reading, May 15 1834, No. 2." 71″ × 47½″. The open rose was a favorite subject for stenciling. (Winterthur Museum)

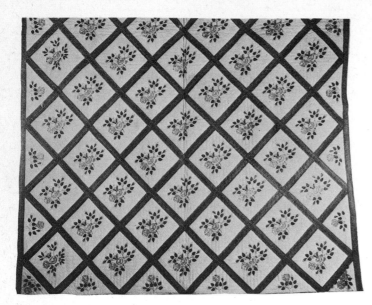

444 (left). Patchwork quilt with stenciled blocks, c. 1850, made by Frances Newbury of Gales Ferry, Connecticut. 90″ × 79″. The blocks are stenciled with an original version of an open rose and are bound together with bands of red calico. (Lyman Allyn Museum)

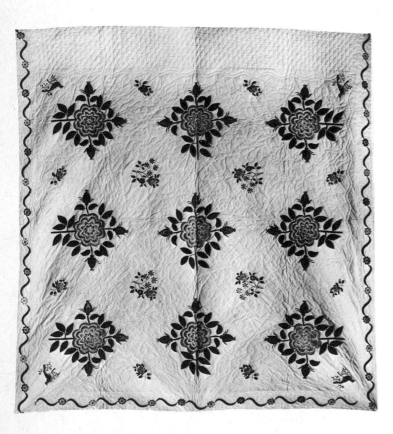

445 (left), 445a (above). Stencil quilt, cotton, c. 1840. 90″ × 78″. All elements of the design are stenciled, and the quilting pattern does much to enhance the total effect of this fine spread. (Henry Ford Museum)

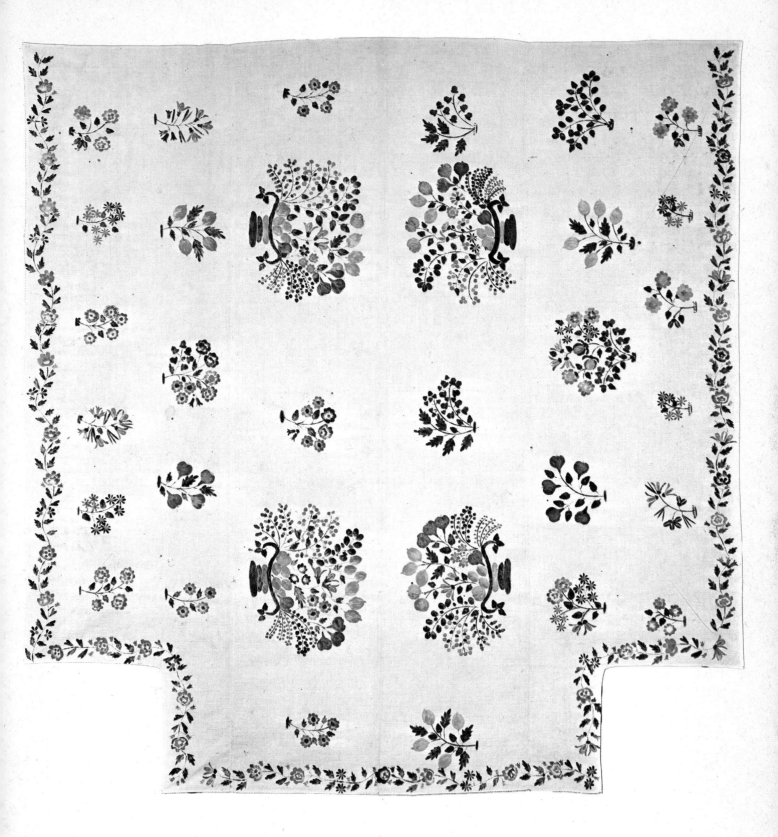

446 (above). Stencil spread, unquilted, c. 1830, New York. 86″ × 81½″. Another beautiful example of stencil work that is particularly interesting for the large baskets of fruit and flowers—a favorite motif in this period of American home arts. The fabric of this spread was spun and woven by Lucinda Howland and decorated by a neighbor in Lisle, Broome County, New York. (Cortland County Historical Society, Inc.)

447 (below). Crazy quilt, appliqué and patchwork, New Jersey, made by Mrs. A. E. Reasoner in 1885. 90" × 88". Mrs. Reasoner was the wife of the Superintendent of what is now the Erie-Lackawanna Railroad. Made of silks and velvets with embroidered details, this fascinating spread shows the route of the railroad through the New Jersey countryside, starting at Hoboken and progressing through Newark, Orange, South Orange, Madison, Convent, and Morristown, all of which are neatly labeled. Note the tiny trains on the tracks and the paddlewheel steamer in the Hudson River at the bottom. (The Newark Museum)

Despite its name, the crazy quilt is usually not quilted, but is finished instead by "tufting" the top, the stuffing, and the lining at regular intervals. At the time of its great popularity in the Victorian period it was used as a "parlor throw" and was primarily meant for show, but it was also useful for a short nap. These throws were of all sizes and weights, shapes and colors. Their principal charm comes from the great variety of embroidery used to embellish them.

The fad for the crazy quilt involved much sentiment, and no house was complete without one for the parlor. The pieces that were sewn together helter-skelter as patchwork were garnered from trunks, relatives, neighbors' wedding dresses, graduation hair ribbons, baby clothes, prize-winner's ribbons, men's ties,—in fact, anything for "remembrance sake" was eligible. Velvet, silk, calico, and wool were used, but no particular pattern was followed. The patch was usually added in the shape that it came to the quiltmaker. The real success of the final "quilt" was not judged by its pattern or a pleasing combination of colors, but by the originality of the embroidery that decorated its surface. Some women with a daring imagination and the ability to draw a little came up with excellent examples of folk art in this medium. Each crazy quilt is individual, for one could collect a thousand and not have any two that were just alike.

Modern collectors of crazy quilts can be selective since there are many specimens still available. However, many connoisseurs of early bedcovers tend to dismiss this type of quilt for not being on a par with other types we have discussed. To quote one on the subject: "Materials were assembled that were never born for each other; its plan of construction suggested the splintered points left by a stone in its passage through a window; pattern it cannot be called, for pattern is ordered relation."

Among the crazy quilts we are illustrating, one in the collection of the Newark Museum is a fine example of the imaginative whimsy shown by the wife of a railroad man. The elaborate use of embroidery, on the other hand, makes an example in the Hennepin Historical Society in Minneapolis a technical masterpiece.

THE CRAZY QUILT

448 (right). Detail from a late-nineteenth century American painting showing a crazy quilt hung over the top of a rocking armchair. (Privately owned)

449 (opposite), 449a (above), 449b (below). Patchwork and appliqué crazy quilt, 1850–1900, made by Miss Celestine Bacheller of Wyoma, Massachusetts. 74¼″ × 57″. The twelve squares that make up this quilt are said to show actual houses, landscapes, and seascapes in the vicinity of Wyoma, Miss Bacheller's hometown. Wyoma was on the north shore of Boston and is now part of Lynn. The quilt is in many colors of silk and velvet and embroidered details are also in multicolored silks. The quilt is bordered with purple plush. One can readily see that the maker made a real attempt to give a sense of perspective in her scenes, even if they did turn out quite distorted. Her quilt, nonetheless, is an outstanding example of American folk art in quilting. (Museum of Fine Arts, Boston; Gift of Mr. and Mrs. Edward J. Healy in memory of Mrs. Charles O'Malley)

450 (left). Silk crazy quilt that is elaborately embroidered, 1884. 75″ × 63″. Initialed "G. W. B." For Rear-Admiral George Washington Baird. (Smithsonian Institution)

451 (below). Silk crazy quilt, dated 1883, from the Roburds family of Vergennes, Vermont. Particularly successful in its overall design and splendid color, this throw also contains a great deal of family history. (Mr. and Mrs. Durand R. Miller)

452 (above). Silk crazy quilt, dated 1883, Albany, New York. 61″ × 61″. Silks, satins, brocades, and velvets are used in this quilt, together with many embroidery stitches. The border of alternating triangles is a most effective finishing touch. (San Antonio Museum Association)

453 (above), 453a (opposite, above right). Crazy quilt, c. 1890, from the Hoskins family of Granville, Vermont. 82″ × 69″. Textures and prints of materials were chosen to represent fur, wavy designs for hair, etc., creating an effective and unusual spread. The designs have been pieced into forty-two separate blocks that were then sewn together. The same method was used in figure 452, so they are not strictly in the "crazy" style. (Shelburne Museum, Inc.)

301

454 (right), 454a (below). Crazy quilt, dated 1887,
Connecticut. 70¾″ × 70½″. Formally speaking, this
extraordinary exercise in patriotism is an appliqué quilt that
has been designed more or less in the crazy-quilt style. The
details are rendered in simple embroidery stitches. The
spread is inscribed in the bottom left corner, "Made by Mrs.
N. W. Carswell, Waterbury, Conn., 1887." On the wide,
black borders at left and right Mrs. Carswell has
embroidered the names of all the Presidents of the United
States up to Grover Cleveland, giving for each his birth date,
the date of his installation as President and his age at the
time, the term of his office, and the date of his death.
(Hudson River Museum)

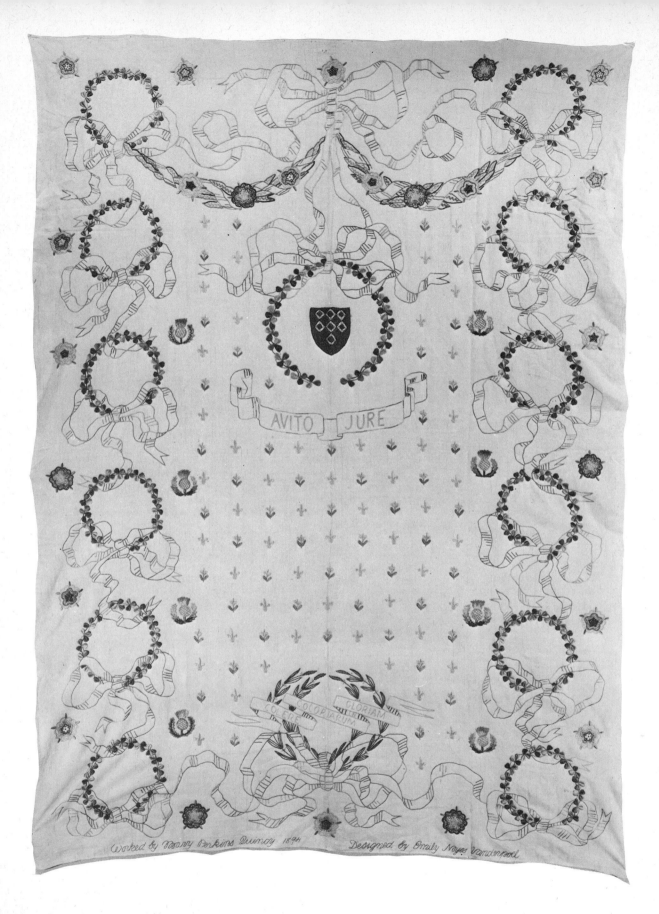

Worked by Mary Perkins Quincy 1894   Designed by Emily Noyes Vanderpoel

455 (above). Spread of homespun linen dated 1794, which
has been embroidered in silk. Made in Litchfield,
Connecticut, in 1894. 95″ × 68″. The spread was designed
by Emily Noyes Vanderpoel, chief benefactor of The
Litchfield Historical Society, and it was embroidered by
Mary Perkins Quincy, an early member of the Daughters
of the American Revolution. (The Litchfield Historical
Society)

456 (opposite). A sample of "historic" embroidery produced
by The Deerfield Society of Blue and White Needlework,
which was active in Deerfield, Massachusetts, in the early
1900's. (Margery Howe)

THE DERIVATIVES

The rapid industrialization of America after the Civil War laid a deadening hand on the once-flourishing home arts. Householders could now buy inexpensively what they used to produce at home, hence they lost most of their incentive to keep the home arts flourishing. It was a period of stagnation and ostentation in the decorative arts. In 1876, however, the Philadelphia Centennial Exhibition, although celebrating America's industrial progress, provided the germ for a rebirth in home crafts by exhibiting handwork by eighteenth-century women, which attracted great admiration.

American women also began to travel abroad, and studied fine Queen Anne embroideries in the English museums. Several English women, under the supervision of The Royal School of Art Needlework, were hired to teach classes in our cities. This was but one of the important antecedents for the growth of interest we are now experiencing in all fields of needlework.

Louis Comfort Tiffany and Mrs. Candace Wheeler organized the first chapter of the Decorative Art Society in New York in 1876. Its purpose was to create a profitable occupation for women with artistic talent. High standards were set and kept, and sales of the work produced by the Society made the project successful. Boston, Philadelphia, and Chicago soon followed suit. In 1878 Boston's chapter met at the Museum of Fine Arts as a School of Needlework. Mrs. Oliver Wendell Holmes, Jr., became renowned as a Boston needlewoman. The famous Mrs. Potter Palmer organized the Needlework and Textile Guild at the Art Institute of Chicago, and in 1891 she was put in charge of the Woman's Pavilion of the Exposition held in 1893.

At about the same time, in Litchfield, Connecticut, a prominent socialite and needlewoman, Mrs. Emily Noyes Vanderpoel, inspired The Litchfield Historical Society to collect old needlework and lace. A commemorative coverlet designed by her, and worked in 1894 by Mary Quincy, is illustrated in this chapter (figure 455).

Two years later (1896) in Deerfield, Massachusetts, two women, Margaret Whiting and Ellen Miller, took the most important step in revitalizing the art and taste that had disappeared during the last quarter of the nineteenth century. Their training of Deerfield women to produce fine weaving and embroidery in the eighteenth-century style resulted in a successful village industry. Both were artists, and they recognized the importance of collecting old fabrics from neighbors' attics. They realized they had rediscovered an invaluable artistic heritage. Miss Miller once said, "The early needlewomen sold their birthright for a mess of sewing machines." As interest in this

457 (above). An example of modern patchwork quilting being displayed on the porch of Mary Dunn's home in Campton, Kentucky. Photograph courtesy Michael D. Hall.

458 (opposite). Mary Dunn of Campton, Kentucky, shows a quilt she made in 1971. This is an original creation, not a copy of an early quilt. Photograph courtesy Michael D. Hall.

project grew, and sketches of old designs filled notebooks, the two women analyzed the various stitches used, sometimes even pulling apart pieces of early embroidery to discover their secrets. Soon other Deerfield women were trained, and the final result was The Deerfield Society of Blue and White Needlework. Margaret Whiting described the project in these words: ". . . to avoid the doubtful value of advertising beyond the intrinsic worth of its output, to demand and get a return which should make the effort profitable; to produce the best possible work, and to spare neither time nor labor nor study to realize that standard."

Linen from Russia, and embroidery thread from Scotland were the basic materials used, and old methods of dyeing were followed. By 1900 thirty trained people were working together. Miss Whiting described the division of income: "The full price of each piece is divided into ten parts: five parts go to the embroiderer; two parts to the designer; two parts to the fund, which is used to pay the running expenses of the society; and the one remaining part covers the expense of materials used." The prices asked amounted to only twenty cents per hour for "trained labor"!

Designs were never duplicated; instead, they were re-adapted or redrawn or stitches were changed. Several women worked together to create sets of bed hangings or curtains. Orders came in faster than they could be filled; other groups started similar businesses, and shops for selling the needlework multiplied and proved profitable. Other early crafts were revived, such as basketweaving, handwrought iron, fire tools, and rugmaking. Miss Whiting's insistence on "theories of good design" appeared

to be the right formula for success. Deerfield prospered, yet fame had its drawbacks. A *New York Sun* reporter wrote: "Living in a tourist center is not entirely joyous and for the sweep of Goths and vandals, the crafts, quite as much as the quaint old Colonial houses and the Indian Massacre traditions, are responsible. Visitors flatten their noses on the living room windows, they even enter and prowl about . . . One householder remarking upon a bevy of craft-hunters, observed that all Deerfield needs is one more good massacre."

The Society continued through World War I, but was disbanded in 1926. The fashion for eighteenth-century home furnishings seemed to be diminishing, and the age of the women who participated made it difficult to maintain steady production.

Fortunately, examples of Deerfield "Blue" have survived and can still be found in antique shops. Their excellent design and workmanship make them worthy of recognition and study. Objects made by the Society can easily be identified by a *D* and a spinning wheel stamped on them.

There has been much recent interest in the art and craft of quilting. Ten years ago a designer-craftsman team, Charles and Rubynelle Counts, moved to Rising Fawn, Georgia, to make pottery. They discovered among their neighbors an amazing wealth of local talent, especially among the women in the rural communities of north Georgia and Alabama. Their skills with textiles had been handed down from Colonial days, and almost every woman was found to be a good quilter. The Counts set about adjusting their own art training to these skills, adapting sizes, colors, and designs to modern household needs. Charles Counts says, "Without that wonderful skill in the hands of these women, our plain designs would be lifeless." The textile mills in the neighboring areas of Chattanooga and Dalton grew out of similar traditional crafts of the cottage-industry type. "The ideas and life are still with the people; and their ingenuity, no matter how commonplace, gives character and beauty to their work. This is what ART is all about and in America we still have some 'from the people' expressions!" So says Charles Counts in a letter giving permission to use some of his designs as illustrations in this book. All the examples are contemporary and influenced by modern art training. The success of the Rising Fawn quilters is assured.

Other successful quilting enterprises include a small group that supplies quilts in an updated style to Design Research in Boston; the Martin Luther King Freedom Quilting Bee, a cooperative organization of about eighty-five black ladies in Gees Bend, Alabama, who make and sell quilts based on old patterns handed down in Southern families; and the Ridge House Side Crafts Association, a small cooperative in Sugargrove, North Carolina, that has sold nearly a million dollars worth of quilts, all traditional in design.

The continuing success of all these groups and others like them is proof enough of the new vitality of and high interest in the needlework crafts, both antique and modern, in our United States.

459 (below). Appliqué quilt, Early Spring Line Storm, 1971, Georgia. 106″ × 90″. Designed by Charles Counts and quilted by Grace Gray and Mrs. Roy Moore. Cotton with dacron quilt batting. (Rising Fawn Quilters)

461 (above). Photograph of Mrs. Roy Moore of the Rising Fawn Quilters in Georgia. All designs for Rising Fawn quilts are drawn freehand directly on the fabric. (Charles Counts)

462 (opposite). Appliqué quilt, Winter Changed to Spring, 1971, Georgia. 102″ × 79″. Designed by Charles Counts in plain cottons with dacron quilt batting. (Rising Fawn Quilters)

460 (left). Detail from an appliqué quilt, Red Quilt, 1970, Georgia. 90″ × 90″. This abstract design by Charles Counts was a Merit Award winner in the first "Appalachian Corridor" exhibition in Charles Town, West Virginia. Quilted by D. Massey and G. Ross. (Rising Fawn Quilters)

BIBLIOGRAPHY

Adrosko, Rita J. "Dye Plants and Dyeing," *Plants and Gardens* (special printing) Vol. 20, No. 3 (Brooklyn Botanic Garden, New York, 1964).

——. *Natural Dyes and Home Dyeing.* New York: Dover Publications, 1971. (originally Smithsonian Institution Press)

Atwater, Mary Meigs. *The Shuttle-Craft Book of American Hand-Weaving.* New York: The Macmillan Co., rev. ed. 1951.

Beer, Alice Baldwin. *Trade Goods, A Study of Indian Chintz.* Washington, D.C.: Smithsonian Institution Press, 1970.

Carlisle, Lilian Baker. *Quilts at Shelburne Museum.* Shelburne, Vt.: Shelburne Museum Publication, 1957.

Chase, Judith Wragg. *Afro-American Art & Craft.* New York: Van Nostrand-Reinhold Co., 1971.

Colby, Averil. *Patchwork.* New York: B. T. Batsford, 1958.

Comstock, Helen (ed.). *The Concise Encyclopedia of American Antiques.* New York: Hawthorn Books, Inc., 1958.

Creekmore, Betsy B. *Traditional American Crafts.* Knoxville, Tenn.: Hearthside Press, Inc., 1968.

Cummings, Abbott Lowell. *Bed Hangings.* Boston: Society for the Preservation of New England Antiquities, 1961.

——. *Rural Household Inventories 1675–1775.* Boston: Society for the Preservation of New England Antiquities, 1964.

Davis, Mildred J. *The Art of Crewel Embroidery.* New York: Crown Publishers Inc., 1962.

——. *Early American Embroidery Designs.* New York: Crown Publishers Inc., 1969.

——. *Embroidery Designs 1780 Through 1820.* New York: Crown Publishers Inc., 1971.

Dooley, W. H. *Textiles for Commercial, Industrial & Domestic Arts Schools.* New York: D. C. Heath, 1914.

Dunham, Lydia Roberts. "Denver Art Museum Quilt Collection," *Denver Art Museum Quarterly* (Winter, 1963).

Earle, Alice Morse. *Costume in America.* New York: The Macmillan Co., 1903.

——. *Customs & Fashions in Old New England.* Williamstown, Mass.: Corner House, 1969. (Reprint of 1893 edition)

Fennelly, Catherine. *Textiles in New England 1790–1840.* Sturbridge, Mass.: Old Sturbridge Village, 1961.

Finley, Ruth. *Old Patchwork Quilts and the Women Who Made Them.* Newton Centre, Mass.: Charles T. Branford, 1971.

Giffen, Jane C. "Household Textiles, a Review," *Historical New Hampshire,* Vol. XXII, No. 4 (New Hampshire Historical Society, Concord, N.H., 1971).

Hall, Carrie A. & Kretsinger, Rose G. *The Romance of the Patchwork Quilt in America.* New York: Bonanza Books, 1935.

Hall, Eliza Calvert. *A Book of Handwoven Coverlets.* New York: Little, Brown & Co., 1912. (1925 edition)

Harbeson, Georgiana Brown. *American Needlework.* New York: Bonanza Books, 1938.

Harris, Estelle M. N. "A Pedigreed Antique," *Antiques* (November, 1927).

Hedlund, Catherine A. *A Primer of New England Crewel Embroidery.* Sturbridge, Mass.: Sturbridge Village Publication, 1963.

Hill, Ralph Nading & Carlisle, Lilian Baker. *The Story of the Shelburne Museum.* Shelburne, Vt.: Shelburne Museum Publication, 1960.

Howe, Margery B. *Deerfield Blue and White Needlework.* Needle and Bobbin Club, Vol. 47, Nos. 1 & 2 (Deerfield, Mass., 1963).

——. *Early American Embroideries in Deerfield.* Deerfield, Mass.: Heritage Foundation, 1963.

Ickis, Marguerite. *The Standard Book of Quilt-Making and Collecting.* New York: Dover Publications, 1959.

Iverson, Marion Day. "Bed Rugs in Colonial America," *Antiques* (January, 1964).

Katzenberg, Dena S. *The Great American Cover-up: Counterpanes of the Eighteenth and Nineteenth Centuries.* Baltimore, Md.: Baltimore Museum of Art, 1971.

Lane, Rose Wilder. *Woman's Day Book of American Needlework.* New York: Simon and Schuster, 1963.

Laury, Jean Ray. *Quilts and Coverlets.* New York: Van Nostrand-Reinhold Co., 1970.

Little, Frances. *Early American Textiles.* Watkins Glen, N.Y.: The Century Co., 1931.

Lord, Priscilla Sawyer and Foley, Daniel J. *The Folk Arts and Crafts of New England.* Philadelphia: Chilton Books, 1965.

MacIver, Percival. *The Chintz Book.* New York: Frederick A. Stokes Co., 1923.

Mayer, Christa Charlotte. *Masterpieces of Western Textiles.* Chicago: Art Institute of Chicago, 1969.

Montgomery, Florence M. *Printed Textiles: English and American Cottons and Linens 1700–1850.* (A Winterthur Book) New York: Viking Press, 1970.

Morris, Barbara. *Victorian Embroidery.* ("Victorian Collector Series.") New York: Thomas Nelson and Sons, 1962.

Morris, William (ed.). *American Heritage Dictionary of the English Language.* Boston: Houghton Mifflin Co., 1969.

Palmer, Frederic. "The Hempsted House," *Antiques* (February, 1960).

Parslow, Virginia D. "James Alexander, Weaver," *Antiques* (April, 1956).

Peto, Florence. *American Quilts and Coverlets.* New York: Chanticleer Press, 1949.

Pettit, Florence. *America's Printed and Painted Fabrics, 1600–1900.* New York: Hastings House, 1970.

Polley, Robert (ed.). *America's Folk Art.* New York: G. P. Putnam's Sons and Country Beautiful Foundation, Inc., 1968.

Preston, Paula Sampson. *Printed Cottons at Old Sturbridge Village.* Sturbridge, Mass.: Sturbridge Village Publication, 1969.

Rabb, Kate Milner. "Indiana Coverlets and Coverlet Weavers," *Indiana Historical Society Publications,* Vol. 8, No. 8 (Indianapolis, 1928).

Schiffer, Margaret B. *Historical Needlework of Pennsylvania.* New York: Charles Scribner's Sons, 1968.

Schwartz, Esther I. "Notes from a New Jersey Collector," *Antiques* (October, 1958).

Sewall, Samuel. *Diary.* Collection of the Massachusetts Historical Society, Series V, Vols. V–VII. Boston, Mass., 1878–82.

——. *Letter Book. Ibid.,* Series VI, Vols. I–II. Boston, Mass., 1886–88.

Stearns, Martha Genung. *Homespun and Blue.* New York: Charles Scribner's Sons, 1963.

Stevens, Napua. *The Hawaiian Quilt.* Honolulu: Service Printers, 1971.

Swygert, Mrs. Luther. *Heirlooms from Old Looms.* Chicago: R. R. Donnelley Corp., 1955.

Whiting, Gertrude. *Old Time Tools and Toys of Needlework.* New York: Dover Publications, 1971.

Wilson, Erica. *Crewel Embroidery.* New York: Charles Scribner's Sons, 1962.

White, Margaret E. *Handwoven Coverlets in the Newark Museum.* Newark, N.J.: Newark Museum Association, 1947.

——. *Quilts and Counterpanes in the Newark Museum.* Newark, N.J.: Newark Museum Association, 1948.

INDEX